spare tire to keep the windshield-washer fluid s...

Remember that scalding blast of sudden heat as the ca...

ur Beetle weighed

$1.02/pound.

Remember when you had to jump-start the car, taking out the backseat since the battery was so *conveniently* located there?

outt sound?

e a double-throated chortler?

Remember waking up after a snooze in the backseat,
and seeing the waffle pattern of the upholstery on your face?

ar, Will Travel.

eople saying that your VW could be pulled along on the
the vacuum created by speeding trucks and buses?

skate?

Remember estimating the amount of gas left
in the tank by watching your mileage?

edited by
MICHAEL J. ROSEN

my bug.

For everyone who owned,

loved, or shared a VW Beetle . . .

true tales of the car that

defined a generation

ARTISAN
NEW YORK

For my brother Gary, who deserves even more than this

Page 157 constitutes an extension of this copyright page.

DESIGNER: Pat Tan

Published in 1999 by Artisan,
a division of Workman Publishing Company, Inc.
708 Broadway
New York, N.Y. 10003

Library of Congress Cataloging-in-Publication Data

    My bug: loving the Beetle in stories and art / edited by Michael J. Rosen.
       p. cm.
     ISBN 1-57965-135-6
     1. Volkswagen Beetle automobile Anecdotes.   2. Volkswagen Beetle automobile
Literary collections.   3. Automobile ownership Anecdotes.   4. Automobiles in art Anecdotes.
I. Rosen, Michael J., 1954–
TL215.V6M93   1999
629.222'2—dc21   99–32504
                                                  CIP

Printed in Singapore
10 9 8 7 6 5 4 3 2 1
First Printing

CONTENTS

INTRODUCTION

BEETLE PEOPLE

GENERALIZATIONS ABOUT ROLLS ROYCE OWNERS or Lambergini owners might be easy to hazard, but it might be slighting to try to characterize Volkwagen Beetle owners. For starters, they cannot be described by wealth or, more importantly, by the lack of it. Having read hundreds of individual accounts of this car and its drivers convinces me that "Beetle People" have shared something like a symbiotic relationship with this vehicle.

Although *My Bug* is an oral history of the most familiar automotive icon in America, it is simultaneously a record of Beetle People, a family of drivers who made this car a part of their family. Beetle People have so many rites of passage in that car—in some cases, the Beetle provided the passage! I suspect that there are more people with more stories about Beetles than might exist for any other car. (It *can* be proven, in fact, that more Beetles have been manufactured than any other car and this, in turn, does make for more Beetle drivers.) Then add to this the fact that a typical Bug remained on the road for longer than the average car, turning its five-figured odometer—99,999 miles—over and over and over. And you have big numbers.

But beyond sheer numbers, Beetle people were—and still are—a different breed. For instance, they don't exactly sound as though they're speaking about cars. I created several books where artists and writers talk about their dogs, horses, and cats, but I thought that taking on an inanimate object—an automobile—might change the nature of the stories. But this collection persuades me that the Beetle's considered an animate object, as natural as anything other creature human beings have bred, groomed, shown, traded, and eventually turned into snow globes, T-shirts, and pewter tchotchkes.

Indeed, a book of 1970s pop psychology by Jean Rosenblum, *Is Your Volkswagen a Sex Symbol?*, claims, and rightly so, that Beetle owners are unique. "When you buy a Volkswagen, you don't just get a car; you also acquire a lot of friends—other Volkswagen owners." The car declares, he suggests, "a certain attitude toward life. . . ." VW people are "concerned about economics, air pollution, and good craftsmanship." They are usually "creative," "intellectual," "rational," and "individualists." His profile concludes by suggesting that VW owners are so loyal to their cars that they do "not harbor secret wishes to own a Cadillac, a Thunderbird, or a Continental."

Clementine. Old Blue. Betty. What other car is so frequently named and nicknamed? Remember the saying? "Our Beetle's a member of the family who just so happens to sleep in the garage." Even when the car wasn't captioned with bumper stickers or stenciled like a rolling billboard with cigarette ads or the floral tresses of the Herbal Essences shampoo bottle, the Beetle itself was the odd shape of a thought bubble, expressing a good deal about the driver inside.

Who would think of painting their Ford Pinto? Who would dream of covering the backside—not just the bumper—of their SUV with bumper stickers, radio station call letters, sun-reflecting peace signs, SDS stickers, and rear-window decals? Beetle People *personalized* their cars; not only did they give their cars some individuality, some personality (remember, at the time, Beetles were ubiquitous and common), but they also conferred a bit of personhood upon the car.

About what other car could Flaubert have written, *"Le coccinelle, c'est moi!"*

No doubt Dean Jones, Michelle Lee, and Buddy Hackett offered more memorable performances during their film careers, but the Volkswagen probably never bested its performance in the *Herbie, the Love Bug* series. Herbie captured something of the nation's growing, shall we say, automotive anthropomorphism. Buddy Hackett's character explains it this way: "Take a car. Most guys will spend more time and money on a car in a week then they do on their wife and kids in a year. Pretty soon, you know what? The machine starts to think it is somebody."

And so rather than recount factory innovations for each year's model, or the Beetles' troubled and still troubling origin (Ferdinand Porsche's original plans, Hitler's commandeering of the car as well as the workforce that concentration camps provided—topics that Peter Aschwanden mentions in his essay), *My Bug* centers on the Beetle as a singularly American phenomenon. The Beetle of the baby boomers, the Beetle of the flower children, certainly, but at less than $2,000, the Beetle was also the choice for students, for young married couples, for anyone just starting out. It was a new driver's first car, the second-hand car inherited from a brother or neighbor, the last car you ever tried to fix yourself.

Beetle People seem to share many stories: having water splashing up through holes in the rusted floor, trying to make out in the front seat—and then the backseat, finding the car reparked down the street after your burly friends lifted it and reparked it as a joke, compacting too many friends inside for that short drive to the Dairy Queen, counting Beetles on a road trip, hoisting the car onto cinder blocks so you could tinker with the brakes.

The Beetle was a bridge, a workhorse, a life raft, a shelter, the jewel in a teenager's crown, a tortoise's shell in which to retreat or travel, or get away or get high. This quirky, egalitarian car was not simply a means of transportation—it was meaning itself.

• • •

Throughout these pages, my brother Gary, who for many years was Gary of Gary's Driveway and VW Repair, answers a few car questions that have, as it were, bugged people over the years. Gary also suggested a few reasons for Beetle People's fierce attachments to their cars. "Not only were they faithful to their cars while they were running—or running over to my driveway for a quick fix-up—a few of my customers never could face the end. When I'd tell them, honestly, sadly, that it just wasn't worth putting any more money into the car, they said, 'OK, I'll just take it home and put it in the garage.' Eight years later, the Bug's still in the garage while the newer car they drive spends winters—and the other seasons too—in the driveway."

Gary's customers were typical: They poured hundreds more dollars into their VWs than the car originally cost them. "This tied in with their belief in recycling: 'Use it up, wear it out, make it last.'

Just as people like to send their Birkenstocks back to the factory to have the soles replaced, Beetle people liked the idea that they were getting their money's worth out of that car, and protecting the environment by not sending it to the landfill."

• • •

The car's adorable shape, its manageable size—not just for parallel parking but for storing in the corner of your parents' driveway—its intimate interior where everything felt within reach, its simple enough mechanisms all inspired allegiance. There was almost no part, no mechanical repair that cost an owner more than $350. The Beetle was worth keeping around.

I can't overlook the fact that many people had less enthusiastic things to say about Beetles. In particular, many Jewish friends, as David Halberstam writes, considered the Bug a Nazi car and can never forgive the Volkswagen's role during Hitler's regime (despite recent news of the company's intention of compensating families of the exploited prisoners). This book in no way mollifies these opinions.

However, in the hundreds of drawings and anecdotes, stories and photographs that follow, is the feeling that the Beetle was a blank canvas, a chance for millions of Americans to imagine something of a future for themselves, however sketchy.

For roughly thirty years—from 1950 to 1980—the Beetle provided the wheels for hope, putting within reach whatever required a car to get a little distance behind the driver or to travel the necessary distance ahead. The Beetle was another word for freedom—as long as you did those oil changes as your older brother advised.

–Michael J. Rosen

THE SHAPE
OF THE FUTURE

For me, its shape has always epitomized the word *improbable*—maybe *goofy* as well. Not armadillolike, exactly, having no tail; not an Inuit igloo, body heat keeping the occupants alive, though it came close to that on a few occasions; not quite a Roswell saucer grown a tad fat and gaseous on New Mexican cuisine, this was an earthbound conveyance that recorded every bump in the road. Primitively modern, somehow, offering no immediate knowledge of whether it was coming or going. We were a year past starting out, a married couple newly in the nest. No need, at long last, for a car to make love in (though we came awfully close at the drive-in a few times, out of habit, if memory serves). We had rented a house and bought a bed, which was not much larger than the car, for that. The shape of the car we bought was the shape of my wife's new body, steeply sloped near and far in ways defying physics. I would usher, shoehorn her into the bright orange Bug carefully, reverently. She was more precious than anything we'd ever come to own, I knew even then. And in time our first child rode in the back in a cardboard box fastened with a belt until we bought a baby seat—our pretty, nearly hairless, portable puppy yipping and da-da-da-ing in back with him.

My father had fought for the west side of Cleveland on Guadalcanal. Later, we'd had to secure his magnanimous victor's acceptance of every one of our Toyotas, until he mellowed in his last years and bought a Honda, but only because it was made in Ohio. Nonetheless, he was Chianti-loud with praise for German engineers. He discounted the rumor he'd heard at the Ford dealership, that Hitler himself had designed this finless toy car. In those days we felt we owned all the time in the world, and then some. We drove an automobile that announced its owners as being young, happy to be cramped together on their way to some sort

of eccentricity, and in no great hurry. These were mean Ohio streets down which our gaudy Beetle skated, more orange than anything we could imagine. We were cold as bone in billows of windy white winter, frost blossoming on the windshield as we learned the dance of the tiny, reluctant clutch, lovers trying to make it to what comes next, baby stuff stowed in front. We bore our treasure proudly from place to place, our hot breaths inches from the flat, tiny windshield, the future chugging toward us like a lawn mower.

—DAVID CITINO
ILLUSTRATION BY ANGELA MATTESON

STONE VW

It was June 1976. (I didn't know at the time that this would be the last year that Bugs were sold in the United States.) At my friend Bill Hill's place in the rural hills near Ithaca, New York, I wandered past the kegs, the crowded horseshoe pits, and out to the woods, where I saw a glowing green knoll. I stumbled upon a stone foundation from a long-vanished farmhouse, grown over by trees. Behind it, I found a round cistern, a well, a square privy,

and, farther back, a pile of fieldstones—everything covered with myrtle. And just down the slope, a worn-out early-sixties VW Bug that Bill had driven into the woods and abandoned.

I had been thinking of building a stone car for some time. I imagined it as a fifties American car, big and square with lots of chrome. I hadn't found the right site. But when I saw that lush setting, the pile of usable stones, and that old Beetle smiling up at me, I knew that this was the right time, place, and car.

The lightness of the Beetle would be a humorous contrast to the heavy and rough stone. The rounded forms of Bug fenders, hood, and roof would be a true challenge to build from rubble—but if I could get that unmistakable Bug profile, it would be recognizable, even from a distance.

I would use the pile of stones to build a lifesize, "dry-laid" Bug, scavenging parts from the real steel Bug, in effect, transforming it to stone. The steel Bug would gradually rust away into the ground, while the stone Bug would remain as a monument.

To keep the tires "full" for centuries, I filled them with concrete, bonding Bug caps and axles. To give the illusion of its floating, I cantilevered large flat stones out over the base, creating running boards and road clearance.

The myrtle aided the effect. The classic VW fenders turned into true stone arches with four rubble boulders as keystones. The windows were slabs of stone found at a local quarry after searching acres of scrap for the right shape. The rear license plate was carved from a block of antique sandstone. And I scavenged a few vintage VW parts: hubcaps, bumpers, wipers, hood insignia, just to add the shine of chrome.

Twenty-plus years later, with the myrtle grown back in, and the stonework muted with moss and lichen, the Stone VW waits in the woods for a time when people will know of the Bug only from the stories like these passed down to them.

—STEPHEN GIBIAN

Most frequently asked question: "Can you get inside?" Alas, no.

HOW I GOT THE BUG IN MY EYE

I saw in a recent filler item in my newspaper that the VW company, with a new Beetle on the road, has announced its intention to compensate its slave laborers of the Nazi era (or, I should hope, their grandchildren) as a moral obligation. For some reason, this brought back a memory of my mother and grandmother around 1950, suddenly speechless at the sight of a Volkswagen in America. They had escaped to Switzerland in 1934 when the Nazis wanted to shoot my grandfather (the feeling, by then, was mutual) so perhaps they had seen the KdF-wagen (Kraft durch Freude, the original Bug name) in the newsreels or *Life* in 1938 when the KdF-stadt (Strength-through-joy city — oh, man) was ceremoniously dedicated as a model workers' town to produce the affordable, air-cooled people's car.

After the speeches, Hitler and rumpled civilian Dr. Porsche were driven off in a prototype cabriolet Beetle before the assembled Hitler youth drum corps, Nazi stuffed shirts, and seventy thousand spectators. This was before the VW factory was turned over to war production and slave labor. Before the destruction of most of it, and of Germany.

After the war my mother sent packages — coffee, rice, soup, soap — to friends and relatives back in Germany. She would buy cartons of Lucky Strikes, I remember, and put them in the boxes to get them into the Soviet zone. American cigarettes in unopened packs represented a stable currency in the occupied zones and, like nylon stockings, changed hands often on the black market. The Reichsmark was, as they say, Kaput.

At about this time in Wolfsburg, to help ease a bombed-out economy, the VW factory workers were cleaning up the mess and beginning to build Kübelwagens for the British into whose zone it all had fallen. From the parts on hand, a few Käfers (Beetles) were assembled but the British were still not interested in getting into the car business there. Not that car.

Recognizable it was, and when my mother and grandmother stopped on the sidewalk, I followed their gaze. The car stood out like a duck in a tiger's cage. In 1950 Detroit iron had swollen fenders and chromium teeth and was just beginning to sprout tits and tail fins: the great American wheeled come-on of the fifties. The Bug had none of this, no hood ornament, no hood at all, just a slope to the bumper, and another slope aft. It was conspicuous in its plainness.

This was it, the car that would help drive the German postwar economy out of its hole. Even so, it must have been like seeing the ghost of Hitler, five years dead, on the streets of Los Angeles.

In the next few years, VW of America played up the economical/comical aspects of the car and after the made-by-elves bumper stickers and giant wind-up keys disappeared there were so many Bugs on the road that they stopped looking like war orphans and by the sixties were moving commuters and transporting much of the counterculture. (Yet the unwary hipster in a VW could still get a bad haircut in parts of Texas or Wyoming.) they were also, I thought, having once driven a thirty-six-horsepower bus over the Rockies to San Francisco, an exercise in patience.

In the autumn of 1969, John Muir and his wife, Eve, showed up at my cabin in New Mexico in a split-window bus. They were working on the manuscript for John's auto repair book for idiots and needed a cover. I had met John once before and had been to his Taos County wedding the previous year — a huge rainy event that ended with the Hog Farm

and friends truck and bus fleet mired to the axles and our own pickup stuck sideways in a ditch on the muddy backroad to El Rito.

John had been a structural Engineer among other things and was now running John's Garage on and off out of his toolbox. He might have become involved with some urban engineering projects such as keeping Manhattan from falling into its own infrastructure, but that would have put him in a hole, I guess. He was more into social structures and VWs and Time — like the timing of our endeavors.

I had just been reading some stuff by John's great-uncle (two greats, I think) John Muir of the mountain, who would climb to the top of a Douglas fir during thunderstorms for a better view, swaying in the wind and who once, after falling off a mountain, lay in the brush cussing out his feet for having grown soft and clumsy on the sidewalks of Oakland.

This was some creative cussing, I thought, the unrestrained statement made in the wilderness. We were fairly dropped out ourselves by then, though I still painted the occasional shop sign for bread. I was, just then, trying to get our goats housed up and firewood in and my wife was drying and preserving produce and tightening up the cabin so that we could make art all winter. A book cover job would buy beans and kerosine.

John and Eve, fired up by the VW book, were writing, drawing, editing, and testing the procedures on amateurs. One of their own work requirements was that they have fun or scrap the project, so when their prospective publishers backed out and took off running, they laughed and took on the publishing as well, selling their Taos house to cover the costs. I think at that time the VW book was for John a vehicle in itself, almost ready to roll, but it wasn't only about cars and he was already eyeing the next thing: a sort of repair manual for society. Big idea, even for the sixties.

In a few days John and Eve came back to see if I would illustrate the text. The drawings were getting more complicated and John needed the time to get the book into production. I pointed out to John that I knew nothing about Volkswagens or mechanics for that matter, and kept a flathead Ford going more with simple hoodoo than by wrenching, and anyway I had to get a roof over my goats before snow. John said that was fine and that I didn't need to read the manuscript, he would just tell me what to draw, leaving the cartoons to me and he would, meanwhile, supply me with pens and smoke and good company between trips to Tosh's in El Rito for technical backup and his typesetting, pasteup, and idiot-testing operations in Santa Fe and Taos.

So there it was. John and I took a

couple of trips to Tosh's place to peer into torn-down VW engines and he came up with pictures, diagrams, parts, and tools as I needed them.

Three weeks later, John and Eve took off for the printer in San Francisco. The book had taken a little longer than John had thought, but he was right about the weather; the barn was finished and I had a copy of *How to Keep Your VW Alive* in my hands before snow flew.

With spring, John and Eve returned. The twenty-five hundred copies were about gone and there were some up-dates to do for the next printing. They had found a book distributor, put the book in *The Whole Earth Catalog* and it started selling. *Rolling Stone* picked it up, which surprised me, since

back then it was a rock and roll and dope mag. *Life* ran a couple of draw-ings and an editorial saying the book wasn't just about cars, pegging it as a love story for our time, and even *The Wall Street Journal* did a num-ber on it because it must have smelled like a trend.

I don't know if all this surprised John but it did give us time to work on some further collaborations, trans-lations, and a seemingly endless timing chart. Time...

John died in 1977 at about the time VW announced that it would no longer produce Beetles in Wolfsburg and that, I thought, was that. I spent the next decade drawing car man-uals for some other imports, all of which have since beached like whales, obsolete and out of print, while the VW book, working on its third mil-lion, keeps keeping on. I guess it wasn't only about cars.

There was a while when I would still see John out of the corner of my mind's eye, looking over my shoulder as I drew those endless mechanical innards. "You can quit, man," he would say, "as soon as you replace yourself," and then he would laugh that sweet laugh of his.

Well— don't set your valves too tight.

—TEXT AND ILLUSTRATIONS
BY PETER ASCHWANDEN

Give me a Brake.

I only had the Volkswagen for a couple of months—during the autumn of 1953 in Paris. One of the editors of the *Paris Review,* Doc Humes, had given it to me. He was on his way back to the U.S. That was the way it was done; you gave a friend any belongings you wouldn't be taking back—a few books, a frying pan, whatever, a car. It was obvious enough why Doc didn't want his car anywhere but off his mind. Painted a somewhat mottled blue, it was very old, maybe one of the first models off the production line . . . surely with a long line of owners before it was passed on to Doc by someone very likely also going home. It worked, but rarely. What I particularly remember about the Volkswagen was an odor it had picked up somewhere, a suffocating smell of putrefaction, as if something quite large had died under the backseat. In fact, that was the usual remark made by anyone taken for a ride, "Hey, what died?" It was best, therefore, to keep the windows open, and the fresh air flowing through, even with winter coming on.

It got me around. I liked the big knob of the gear shift. But I always got into the Volkswagen feeling something was going to go wrong, and at my destination I always got out relieved that nothing untoward had happened, like the engine falling out into the street.

Once, when it was creeping down the Boulevard Raspail, the car's brakes gave out, I pushed the brake pedal and it went straight to the floor—apparently not a drop of hydraulic fluid in the system. I was moving about ten miles per hour. I opened the door and dragged my foot along the cobblestones, slowly bringing the car to a halt—already in my mind what I was going to say in my tortured French if I bumped into someone from behind. "*Je suis désolé. Ma voiture n'a pas l'abilité à quitter."*

I passed on the car to someone else when I came back to the U.S. later that year. He was a newcomer in Paris, just arrived from Boston. He didn't know. He couldn't believe his luck.

"A car? I'm so damn grateful."

"Not at all," I said.

I suppose I must have smiled.

—GEORGE PLIMPTON

23

FROZEN BUG

The Bug was notorious for its erratic heater. It worked well when the engine strained to get up hills. Heat poured from the vents. But when the Bug tooled along on flat roads or going downhill, the heater barely whispered warmth.

Winter 1968. My friend Duncan and I decided to rendezvous with friends at Mount Mansfield in Vermont from our homes in Amherst, for a long weekend of skiing.

As fate would have it, when we set out that Friday morning it happened to be the coldest day of the winter, which meant it would only get colder the farther north we went. When Duncan picked me up, the air temperature was hovering somewhere around the five-degree mark.

We set off toasty warm but within half an hour, the chill had begun to seep into our little cab. The defroster was barely breathing. My job was to use the ice scraper on the inside windshield and windows. By the time we arrived at the inn, some three hours later, skiing was no longer our top priority. Though we didn't spend the whole long weekend hunkered by the inn's fireplace, we defrosted ourselves there for quite some time.

**—TEXT AND ILLUSTRATIONS
BY CHRIS DEMAREST**

"Coochie-coochie
Coo"

THINKING SMALL

In 1959, Doyle Dane Bernbach, a New York advertising agency, began its campaign for Volkswagen of America, and over the next twenty years, created one of the best recognized, most successful, and profoundly influential ad campaigns in history.

The traditional way to sell automobiles, whether in print, in the car lot, or on the new television, featured every sort of hyperbole, enticement, and bravado. Cars were often obscured with streamers, singers, pageantry, and the other appurtenances of hype and hoopla. Dealerships staged mini-carnivals, offered free refreshments, booked clowns and other sideacts (my favorites were to come see a man buried alive and a woman frozen in a block of ice). Detroit was varying the design of cars each year, varying the detailing, appending boots, fins, bonnets, and so forth: Cars were sold like designers' fashion, and fashion sold cars.

Enter the Beetle ads. They were simple, clean, straightforward, ingenuous, and realistic. They lacked the constantly employed artistic air-brushing and enhanced photographic effects. No fetching models posed beckoningly beside the car. No fancy typography, inventive layouts, or dramatic narratives. Beetle ads were quiet, disarmingly plainspoken, and almost irreverently self-conscious—all of which was totally unheard of in car advertising.

The VW Beetle ads focused on the accessibility of repair parts, its winter driving strength, great mileage, low price, the obsessive factory inspections, or how each year's car modifications shouldn't be about restyling so much as about fine tuning.

Those black-and-white photographs with the consistent sans-serif type underneath became fixed in the consumer's mind. The photographs simply portrayed a Beetle, front and center, with no background to suggest anything specific: just the car on that curved white photographer's psyche. The captions were the same. Some favorites:

"Ugly is only skin-deep."

"Don't let the low price scare you off."

"Live below your means."

"After a few years, it starts to look beautiful."

"Do you earn too much to afford one?"

"Lemon" ("This Volkswagen missed the boat. The chrome strip on the glove compartment is blemished and must be replaced. Chances are you wouldn't have noticed it. Inspector Kurt Kroner did. There are 3,389 men at our Wolfsburg factory with only one job: to inspect...")

"Think small." (This time the car is simply farther away, smaller, and higher on the page.)

"It makes your house look bigger." (The car in smaller profile, positioned on the page about where it might be parked in front of a house, were it there.)

"$1.02 a pound." ("A new Volkswagen costs $1,595. But that isn't as cheap as it sounds. Pound for pound, a VW costs more than practically any car you can name.")

And here are a few favorite ads that did include more than just a photograph of the car:

"A common misconception about air-conditioning old Volkswagens." A bulky room air conditioner protrudes from the passenger's window.

"Volkswagen's unique construction keeps dampness out." The Bug is floating in a clear tank of water.

"They said it couldn't be done. It couldn't." (Seven foot one inch tall, Wilt "The Stilt" Chamberlain stands by the open car door.) "No amount of pivoting or faking could squeeze the Philadelphia 76er's Wilt Chamberlain into the front seat of a Volkswagen."

The ad campaign was so unmistakable that one ad dropped an image altogether. On an otherwise blank page, the same simple type block at the bottom quarter reads: "No point showing the '62 Volkswagen. It still looks the same."

RUM-RUNNING

I'm somewhat ashamed of this story, but my bootlegging was a matter of survival, sort of, and my 1961 VW was perfectly suited for rum-running.

I bought it used while I was in college at the University of Texas at Austin in the fall of 1966. It was one of the old versions without a fuel gauge. There was a handle on the upper floorboard under the dash that you turned with your foot when you ran out of gas. The spare tank gave you an additional gallon, probably thirty to thirty-five miles more.

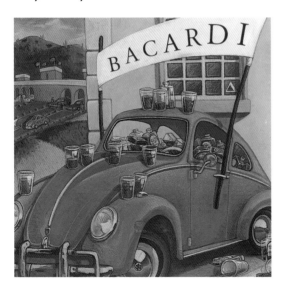

I was returning the handle back to its upright position after a fill-up one day when I discovered that the right footrest on the passenger side of the car was at about a forty-five-degree angle. What seemed odd to me was that when you tapped it, there was a hollow sound. I pulled up the rubber matting and discovered a metal plate with a finger hole in it. When I raised the plate, there was a fairly sizable vacant area behind it quite suitable for storage. As it turned out, two liter bottles of Bacardi fit nicely into the secret compartment.

At the time, my hometown was Del Rio, Texas, located along the Mexico border. Alcohol was extremely inexpensive in Mexico, having none of the U.S. taxes. I was buying liter bottles of Bacardi rum (a favorite of college students then) for about $2 apiece (16 pesos in those days) in Mexico and selling them for $8 to $10 in Austin.

My importing began modestly, I smuggled a bottle or two through the customs guards when I was home on the holidays. The resale of the bottles would usually pay for my gasoline for the trip home (gasoline was 26¢ a gallon) and a couple of bucks for a dinner. Smuggling was always risky—not so much from the legal standpoint as from the risk of the customs guards calling your parents. (Del Rio was pretty small and everyone knew everyone else. If a Del Rio kid was caught doing something illegal, a call was made to the parents rather than the Feds.)

That summer before my junior year, I began running two bottles of Bacardi back over to the American side each time I visited Mexico (which was fairly often since I was not yet twenty-one and in Mexico you could drink if you had a quarter for the beer). By summer's end, I had amassed nearly four cases of Bacardi for an investment of about $70, clearing a profit of about $250—enough to pay for my tuition and books for the semester. I continued my business well into my senior year until my Bug burned up an engine and needed a replacement. I traded it in for a much more sporty Dodge Dart—big mistake. The Dart was never the car my Bug was, nor did it have the necessary accoutrement for a successful rum-retailing business. My rum-running days were over. I never owned another Bug, and I doubt it would have the same feel for me now as it did then. Also, I now buy my rum retail.

—ROBERT INDERMAN

ILLUSTRATION BY MICHAEL PHILLIPS

FRANKENBEETLE

My parents had a succession of VW Beetles in the 1960s. My two brothers and I used to fight over who would get to ride in the tiny space behind the backseat. Of course, in the summer, it wasn't such a prime spot; it was hot as hell in there with the engine below and the sun beating in through the back window. If you jumped into the car with shorts and short sleeves on, any area of exposed flesh that came into contact with the molten plastic seat would instantly be seared off.

After a long evening visit with friends in the dead of winter, my parents would load my brothers and me, shivering and sleepy, into a backseat then frozen as hard as steel.

31

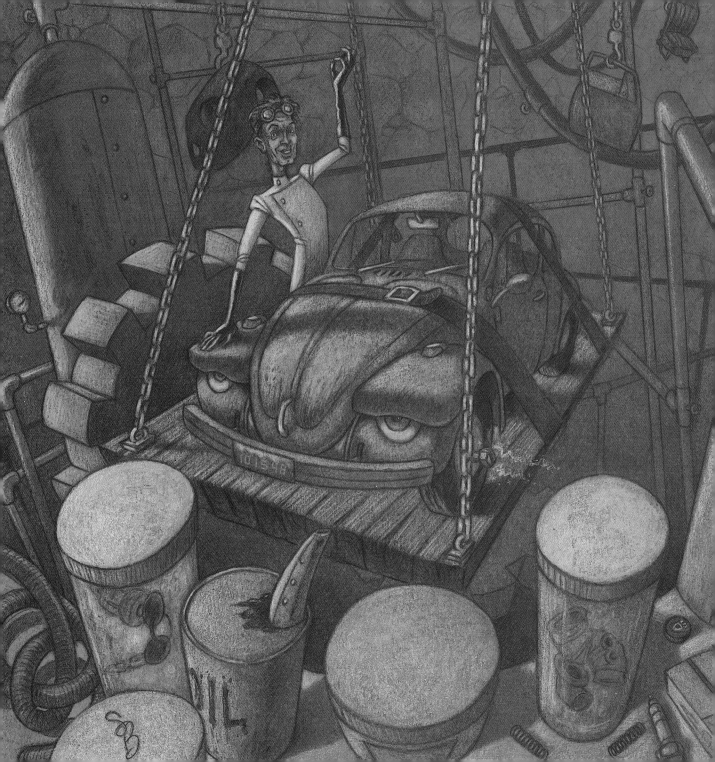

It always took at least fifteen minutes of driving to get the engine warm enough to blow any heat into the car, and by then we were nearly home. The best spot was in the middle. That way, you could absorb the meager heat emitted by the brother on either side, while avoiding the direct exposure to the vents down by the floor on each side of the car. Once the engine got hot, those vents would put out superheated air like a blowtorch, charring your feet while your butt went numb from frostbite on the arctic seat.

Memories of the manic nature of Bug heating and cooling didn't affect my brother Tom. At any given time in his teens and early twenties, Tom had two or three Beetles on hand. Most of his free time was spent tearing one apart or putting one back together.

In fact, whatever Beetle he was driving was composed of pieces scavenged from several others. Sometimes you could tell how many by the different colors of the fenders. The cars were bolted together into something that actually would chirp to life and move.

Sort of a FrankenBeetle.

—**GLENN SHELLER**
ILLUSTRATION BY SCOTT BROOKS

WHAT'S THAT BEETLE SMELL?

OUR RESIDENT MECHANIC EXPLAINS
by Gary of Gary's Driveway VW Repair

Q: Why do Beetles smell like Beetles?

A: Beetle seats are stuffed with natural sisal, the stuff used for making twine. I gather it comes from some kind of agave plant, and it shreds into cords or fibers, kind of like hemp—although it can't be too much like hemp, or lots of Beetle owners would have come to me over the years to restuff their seats. Anyway, when it warms up (I don't mean the car, just the weather), or when moisture gets in the seats, the sisal "gasses," and gives off that characteristic odor. But, come on, it's not a bad smell. It's not like you see Beetle owners hanging piña colada air fresheners from the rearview mirror.

I drilled a hole in the center of the roof and installed an amber light so truckers could see us passing. Sarah (9) said, "that thing is going to leak." It did.

Dione was always asking me to stop then she would dig up some wild flowers and plop them in the VW. When we finally sold the car for a dollar the new owner shoved the passenger seat forward — there was a nice assortment of green stuff growing in a bed of mud and water on the floor. Lordy.

G. Booth.

ACCIDENTS WILL HAPPEN

The fall of 1968 I turned sixteen, dyed my hair blond, and acquired my first VW Bug. I learned to drive that fall by motoring in circles around my parents' front lawn, which, while a substantial size, did not provide a chance to go beyond second gear. The following February I had my first accident.

My best friend, Nancy, and I did everything together, including having our roots done at the beauty shop. As Nancy was being combed out, they took me from under the heat machine that activated the chemicals applied to my hair. The beautician began to comb, and my hair started falling out in disturbingly large clumps. When she finished, to my horror, there were still some strands of hair that made it to my chin, but most of my hair was less than an inch long!

The beautician suggested I wear a wig until my hair grew long enough for a decent haircut. For the next month, me and my blond bouffant became close friends.

Two weeks later on the way home from the supermarket with hamburger and buns for a sloppy joe dinner in hand, I gravely miscalculated a turn. Crossing three lanes of southbound traffic to make a left-hand turn

into the northbound lanes during rush hour was a little too ambitious. Halfway across the road I had to stop to avoid hitting another car making a left-hand turn from the main roadway. Unfortunately, a car heading south didn't see me sitting there until it was too late. It struck my right front fender, sending my Bug spinning in a circle. Partway through the spin, the driver's door opened and somehow I managed to fall out onto the roadway. Dazed but seemingly in one piece, I stood up only to witness my Bug jumping over the curb and heading off toward the Drug Fair without me. I began chasing it, yelling, "Somebody please stop my car!"

By now the Bug made a ninety-degree turn and was at least heading parallel to all the parked cars in the Drug Fair lot rather than straight for them. To my enormous relief, it then made another ninety-degree turn and abruptly stopped at the curb.

A U.S. Parks policeman got to me first. I was standing next to my now stationary Bug when he came up, saying he would call an ambulance immediately. I said that wasn't necessary, I was a little shaky but all right. He looked at me quizzically and said, as if not to upset me any further, that I had blood pouring down my forehead. I glanced in my rearview mirror and saw that somehow, even though the Safeway bag was still in the car, hamburger juice had spattered all over me. Just as I turned around to reassure the policeman that it was hamburger juice not blood, the policeman reached over to check my nonexistent wound, knocking my wig askew and causing a gasp from the gathering crowd that was sure I had been scalped.

I never bleached my hair blond again, but I ended up owning two more Bugs and a VW bus!

—SHIRLEY GROMEN
ILLUSTRATION BY JOHN YANOK

Illustration by D. Kohler

Nineteen sixty-four or thereabouts. It was a small car of nondescript color, owned by several, borrowed by many, and loved by more than a few. In the end, all that remained were third gear and reverse. With some difficulty, it was driven to a remote beach on the Atlantic coast. At the edge of the water, its choke and throttle were pulled out. Slowly, and alone it made its way into the ocean and disappeared from sight.

Later, there were reported sightings in South America, although none was confirmed.

—TEXT AND ILLUSTRATION BY VICTORIA CHESS

HMMZ

License plate: HMZ135. "Hmmz," I called it. Yes, it. I never designated Hmmz male or female, after all it wasn't a battleship or a luxury liner—except maybe in spirit. Ginger, my car pool buddy, thought the comparison should be more aeronautic than nautical: a kamikaze plane that offered two subtle forms of suicide: the first, merging into high-speed traffic on the Hollywood freeway like some bug (pun intended) blithely sniffing its way across a busy sidewalk; the second, death by asphyxiation. With the heater on we risked suffocation if at least two windows weren't partially rolled down.

On rare occasions, Hmmz caught fire. I never took it personally. I carried extra hose clamps after the first fire, lesson learned. My favorite repair tool, however, was an emery board. If Hmmz's engine wouldn't start, all I had to do was open up the trunk and hold an emery board parallel to the ground, slipping it between the points and filing ever so carefully, top then bottom. Hmmz appreciated the fact that I knew these sensitive areas and had a gentle touch.

It was the fashion, in Southern California, to transform one's V-dub into a rolling billboard, mostly for tobacco companies. I couldn't bring myself to strip Hmmz of its dignity like that. Hmmz would have been insulted and our relationship would have cheapened if I let it be painted like some tawdry side-show performer. I respected Hmmz for the tough hills it climbed, the tiny parking spaces it fit into, and its meager gasoline appetite. I treated it with respect and it did my bidding.

When my godchild Pat packed up her room and moved to college, I sent her off in my beloved Hmmz with a reminder, "I want it back after you're done using it." It did tug at my heart though, watching this child who was like my very own, who had shared my home for years, just drive away. "There they go," I said to no one. "I'm really going to miss that car."

—LESLIE TRYON

ILLUSTRATION BY MARIANO SANTILLAN

A FEW MEMORABLE MOMENTS IN THE BEETLE'S LIFE HISTORY

Illustration by D. Kohler

1935

Ferdinand Porsche creates a car that will become the prototype of the Beetle.

1936

Porsche delivers the so-called ugly duckling to Hitler, who has commissioned the first automobile for the working class.

1938

The New York Times, using the word "beetle" in reference to the new German car for the first time, coins the Beetle nickname.

The city of Wolfsburg lays the foundation of a production village. Hitler initiates coupon books, which each German citizen can use to buy a Beetle, pasting in stamps in order to buy a car at the factory. (Approximately 5 marks a week—plus an additional mark for insurance—allows the citizen to buy a Beetle, in about three years, for 990 marks, or something like $400 by today's standards.)

1939

The VW plant is converted for wartime production, redesigning the car for military purposes: the Kübelwagen, or "bucket car," (much later, a modified version was marketed as "The Thing"), as well as the Schwimmwagen, an amphibious car with four-wheel drive and a propeller on the rear of the car to move it through water. Survivors of the detention camps are recruited as the labor force.

1945

Having sustained heavy bombing during the war, the plant lies in ruins. Porsche is imprisoned. Eventually, the British manage to put the factory back on line. First, post office delivery vans are produced. Then the British invite Heinz Nordhoff, who managed the Opal car's production, to begin building Volkswagens again.

1948

Twenty thousand Beetles so far have rolled off the production line in Germany. Heinz Nordhoff comes to America to speak with Dave Garraway about the Beetle on an equally novel machine, the television.

1949

The British give the car's production back to the German government, and the first two cars are sent to New York City.

1950

The first car importer, Maximilian E. Hoffman, receives twenty cars in New York City. The prices: Volkswagen Standard, $1,280; Volkswagen Deluxe, $1,480; Volkswagen Deluxe with Sunshine Roof, $1,550; Volkswagen Convertible, $1,997.

1952

The Beetle's window cranks now require only three and a half instead of ten and a half turns to lower the window.

1955

A total of five hundred thousand Beetles have been produced to date. Nearly thirty one thousand sell this year in the United States alone. For the first time, demand outstrips supply, and people need to wait for the arrival of their new cars.

1958

The tiny oval window in the rear is enlarged.

1959

One of the most successful and memorable advertising campaigns in history begins. Doyle Dane Bernbach creates its straight-forward, honest, witty approach using simple black-and-white photography, plain typography, and self-consciously earnest copy.

1962

The gas gauge finally appears! No more worries from guessing whether the car has enough gas to make it to a filling station.

1965

Nine hundred Volkswagen dealerships are operating in America, serving two million Beetle owners.

1966

Flower power co-opts the Beetle as its roving billboard with appliqué flowers, peace signs, and bumper stickers protesting America's increasing involvement in Vietnam.

1967

Factory-installed seat belts arrive.

1968

More Volkswagens are sold this year than any other: 567,975. A semiautomatic gearbox is offered for the first time to attract other buyers.

1971

The Super Beetle is introduced, along with the VW 411, a four-door sedan, and a companion station wagon.

1972

A special Super Beetle, the Baja Champion SE, is introduced with desert racing features such as metallic paint, pressed steel wheels, and fog lights for the front bumper.

1973

The threat of gas rationing, as well as long lines at filling stations, give Beetle owners a chance to gloat over their great mileage. The

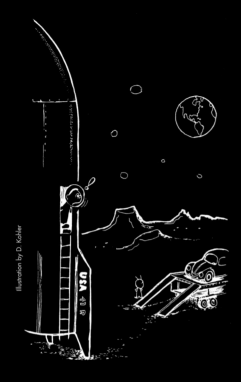

Illustration by D. Kohler

1977

Stricter emission-control measures and safety standards begin to depress sales, and Volkswagen declares this to be the last year for the Beetle in the U.S.

1978

The last German-built Beetles roll off the assembly line. (Convertibles continued for another year.)

1994

Volkswagen unveils its modern-day Beetle, the Concept, at the Detroit Auto Show.

1998

Volkswagen releases the first of the new Beetles. The next wave begins with slogans such as More Power. Less flower.

2000

At the turn of the millennium, the Volkswagen Beetle turns sixty-five years old. (Owners can apply for retirement.)

basic Beetle still sells for under $2,000. The Thing arrives, sells for a couple of years, and then is pulled from the market in 1975.

1975

The Beetle's carburetor is replaced by a fuel-injection system. "No lead" gasoline is required. The "Old Faithful" Beetle is shown with Volkswagen's latest hope, the water-cooled Rabbit, the "New Faithful."

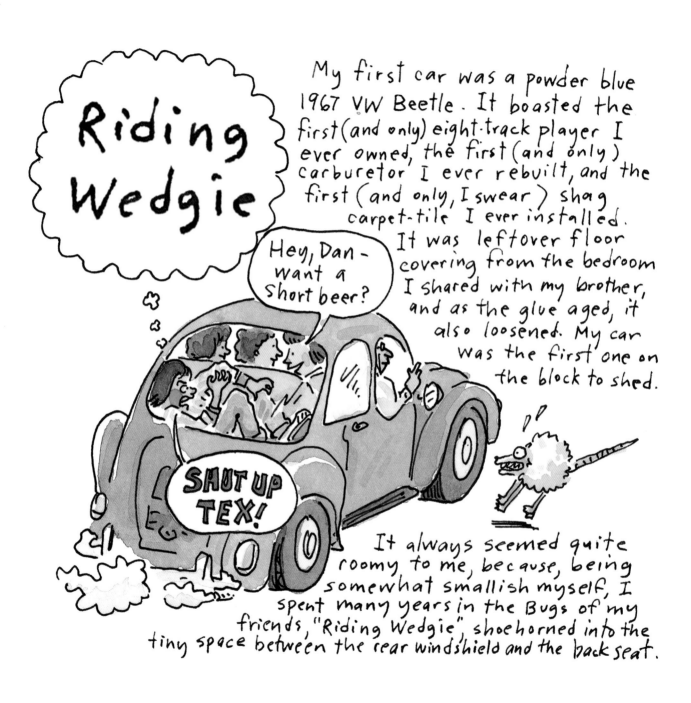

We were all Beetle owners: Brother Bernie, Danny Wildman, Paul "Tex" McCahill, Kilto Bud. VW ownership was a rite of passage. On Friday evenings we'd all pile into one car (strictly a financial decision - less money for gas = more money for beer), and cruise from barn party to open field, basement to bonfire.

No nocturnal woodland creature was safe. Tooling around on the notoriously winding country back roads of Northwestern Connecticut, we'd have to constantly brake or swerve to avoid the many little pairs of glowing eyes. Some of our animal encounters grew to legendary proportions. People still talk about the Phantom Beaver of Flanders Turnpike. But that's a different story...

—TEXT AND ILLUSTRATION BY DANNY SHANAHAN

THE DAY MY KEY CHAIN CAUGHT FIRE

People who have driven a VW convertible for a while know it's a car with a sense of humor. Some things are straightforward: starting, steering, and shifting are done in a quite familiar manner, though finding reverse can be amusing for the neophyte, especially since the helpful picture on the dashboard is ridiculously misleading.

But the car's designers lavished their Teutonic humor more opulently on the secondary functions: turning on the defroster, opening the hood, filling the windshield washer, putting on the tonneau cover, getting a jump start from another car.

The jump start, for example, is good sport in any weather and especially diverting in the rain, since the battery is located under the backseat, a large slablike bench that is quite hard to remove when the top is down—i.e., when you can stand up and get some purchase on the thing—and nearly impossible with the top up—when you have to crouch in the tiny foot well and wiggle the seat up and out. Then, of course, you have to put it outside in the rain (so good for the seat stuffing) and snake the cables through the front door—while the front seat is getting wet too—to the battery in the rear. Who says Germans don't know how to have fun?

And is there another car on earth with a more baroque heater/defroster system? Two levers, two unlabeled flap knobs, and an unlabeled fan knob. Hundreds of combinations are possible, and, at least in my car, not one of them will defrost the driver's side. Then there's the windshield squirt mechanism. I imagine a contest among the Volkswagen engineers to join this function in the most bizarre way to some other part of the car.

"Well, how about putting a bladder under the driver's seat?"

"*Nein, nein,* too simple."

"Attach it to *das* radio! To clear the windshield, you must play *De Walkürie* at full volume!"

"*Ach . . . besser,* but some models have no radio."

"I know. Attach it to the spare tire!"

"*Wunderbar.* Gentlemen, we have a winner!"

Just when I had grown used to all this, the key chain caught fire. It was a pleasant afternoon in the early 1980s, and I was driving, top down, through a pretty village on the coast of Maine when I smelled smoke and, at thirty miles an hour, found that the wooden toggle, cunningly made to resemble a lobsterman's float, was ablaze, like a bright little match. I swerved to the curb, blew it out, and with no particular forethought, tried to turn the engine off. If I had taken a second I would have reasoned that a wooden object at the end of a chain caught fire because the chain was hot, and the chain was hot because the key itself was hot. But I didn't, and I burned my fingers and said several unmentionable things before wadding up a handkerchief and silencing the car.

There is no particular punch line to the story, unless it occurred that night at dinner when my mother solemnly gave me a new accessory for my car: a pot holder. The local mechanic had several theories, but the event never recurred, so they remain theoretical. I did get a fire extinguisher and bolted it in plain sight. I still have my mother's pot holder, the key chain with its singed float, and no explanation. Maybe it goes along with the squirt mechanism that deflates the spare tire; maybe the key ring is wired to the spark plugs; maybe this is supposed to happen. It remains a mystery.

—ROBIN CLEMENTS
ILLUSTRATION BY ELIZABETH HORNBECK

Forward or Backward?

I remember my first impressions of the VW Beetle when it began showing up in Cambridge around 1952. That was the perfect place for it. Two debates waged simultaneously around Harvard: The first question was, Which direction is the car heading? And the second question, which also plagued potential Mercedes owners: Is it all right for a person who is Jewish to buy such a car?

At least one answer has become clear: The Beetle was heading toward becoming the first Yuppie car.

—DAVID HALBERSTAM

SPECKLED, RUSTED, SALTED, BATTERED, BLISTERED, TRUSTY BUG

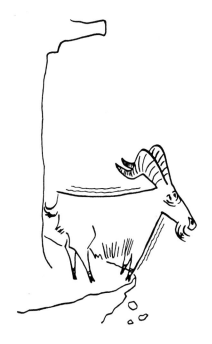

I took a long hard look at my Volkswagen in 1976 when I decided to move from Tuscaloosa to Syracuse. The one thing I knew about Syracuse was that the winters were brutal, and the locals salted the roads as if they were the rims of the world's largest margarita glasses. A lot of rusty metal already scabbed the paint of my 1969 Bug. It didn't need any more.

I had learned how to drive in this car, and I had learned slowly. When I was eighteen, I smacked the protective stanchion at a 7–Eleven and banged a big dent into the right front fender. The entire left side of the car sported a deep rusty gouge. (Who'd have thought that loading dock was sticking out so far?) And stone chips speckled the roof and hood because rather than back off and let gravel trucks get well ahead of me, I always tried to pass them. Since Volkswagens and fully loaded gravel trucks possess nearly equal powers of

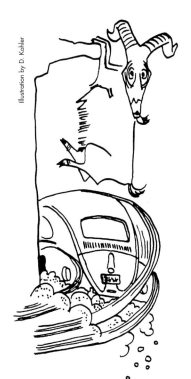

Illustration by D. Kohler

49

acceleration, I drove many miles of back-road Alabama listening to the crack of stone against sheet metal. Even across a crowded mall parking lot, I had no trouble identifying which blue VW was mine.

And the picture that my little brother drew on the passenger door with a nail? It was a square house with a front door, two windows crisscrossed with muntins, and a chimney. A whimsical wisp of smoke curlicued from the chimney. It took me about two years to share my family's amusement with the house, and another two to become fond of it.

I could think of only one way to protect my car from salty northern roads. I drove to the True Value Hardware store, planning to purchase twenty spray cans of blue Rustoleum. But at the store, daunted by the price of the spray cans, I bought two quarts of paint and a two-inch brush. Within three hours, working in the driveway of my apartment, I had the car painted. The next day, because I had some paint left over, I brushed a second coat on the worst spots. I wouldn't have had the courage to paint any other car in the world, but the Volkswagen was worth maybe $400. What difference did some brush strokes make?

Very little, as it turns out. Within days, the paint began to slough off the car in strips. I hadn't known to roughen the surface of the old paint with sandpaper so the new coat would stick to it. Friends began to exercise their vocabularies on my mistake. Leprous. Scrofulous. Syphilitic. Loud retching noises were a popular witticism. I got a little hot only when the phrase "white trash" cropped up.

Despite its looks, the car made it through two winters in Syracuse before I moved back to Alabama. In Montgomery, nobody in my lower-middle-class neighborhood said anything about this eyesore parked on the street. But as we talked, their eyes kept flicking over to it unhappily. By then the entire top coat of medium-blue Rustoleum, brittle and blistered from two summers under the broiling Alabama sun, was peeling off in sheets, revealing large patches of the battered navy blue beneath it.

Finally my next-door neighbor said to me, false casually, "You know, if you want to paint that thing, I could help you out. I got a compressor and a spray gun out in my shop back of the house."

For two solid days in ninety-five-degree August heat, I sanded the car with wet and dry sandpaper. Using progressively finer grits, I feathered the Rustoleum into the original paint and raw metal, sanding until I couldn't feel any seams. Then I slathered Bondo into the dents and gouges, let it dry, and sanded some more. By dumping together all the leftover bits of paint he had in his shop, my neighbor mixed up a batch of cheap primer and painted the car battleship gray. I spent another afternoon sanding the primer before I drove downtown to an auto supply store and bought, for $30, a gallon of "Volkswagen blue." That night my neighbor sprayed the car, restoring it to its original color.

The next morning, Saturday, I discovered why he had been so generous. His air compressor thumped on at 6:15, as it did every subsequent Saturday that I lived next to him, jerking me out of sleep weekend after weekend. He'd gone into the auto painting business as a sideline. But after all his help, I was in no position to complain—he knew it and I knew it.

With only a few drip lines on the sides and around the headlights, though, the car looked terrific. So I sold it for $1,000, exactly what my father had bought it for ten years earlier. Two months after I transferred title to the new owner, a girl in one of my classes said to me, "Are you the guy who sold that blue VW Bug to Linda?"

"Yeah," I said.

"Well, it's on its way to Texas right now, even as we speak. It's probably in Louisiana already."

Going to Texas! The car I'd driven to Syracuse then back to Alabama. The car I'd flogged all over north Florida when I was a Nabisco salesman. Now bright blue again and packed to the ceiling, it was on the road to Texas.

"Good for it," I thought. "I wish I were going too."

—ANDREW HUDGINS

ILLUSTRATION BY JENNIFER EMERY

Warhol's Side.

My very first car was a Beetle, a red one, back in the early sixties. I bought another one in 1979—the last year they made the originals—when I finally began to support myself as a writer in San Francisco. I remember how vulnerable those little side windows were. Someone popped mine out once and stole a leather jacket when I was at a sex club called the Glory Holes. A week or so later, I was driving Andy Warhol around town, and the wind from the missing window was ruffling his wig something fierce. "What happened here?" he asked in a voice that could somehow sound both interested and disinterested at once. When I told him about the theft, he forgot about the Beetle altogether and wanted a complete rundown on the Glory Hole—an institution I'm sure he understood already. Andy was a sort of Listening Tom: He got off on hearing other people describe sexy things. I thought of that recently when Barbara Walters pretended not to know what phone sex was so she could make Monica Lewinsky describe it.

—ARMISTEAD MAUPIN

FLOAT SOME, JET SOME

OUR RESIDENT MECHANIC EXPLAINS
by Gary of Gary's Driveway VW Repair

Q: Why do Beetles float?

A: All well-made cars will float because the interior is supposed to be well sealed. That's what keeps the noise out. That's what makes the car sound like a concert hall auditorium.

In the Beetle era—the fifties, sixties, and seventies—the other auto manufacturers' cars simply weren't airtight. But then, neither were houses at the time. In fact, everything was drafty then, including the war in Vietnam.

But Beetles were different. Maybe some of the watertightness was left over from when Hitler had the factory design an amphibious version of the early Beetle for wartime use (it didn't submerge like a sub, but it did have a propellor in the rear for scooting across streams). That car was watertight. So much for wartime wonders.

Decades later, VW ran ads that showed how you had to crack open a Bug's window in order to shut the door. That was one of the quirky things they bragged about. Beetles eventually do sink, but they are also small, round, and lighter than most cars, so they have some extra buoyancy.

LE COCCINELLE *

A colleague of mine at Georgetown College in Kentucky drove what I think was a King Midget—a tiny contraption cobbled together out of tin sheeting, isinglass, and canvas. When I rode to school with her one day, I felt not only vulnerable, but apologetic; we were scrunched down low on the street, as if looking up the skirts of tractor trailers.

But that wasn't a car; nobody thought it was. At best, it was a vehicle, a device whose function was to get her the few blocks from home to school and become the object of a search at the end of the day, since students couldn't resist picking it up and moving it about the campus.

Cars back in 1957 were big, powerful, and heavy with metal, as they had remained for many years despite a few attempts at reduction. In 1938, for instance, my father bought a Ford 60, a faltering step toward diminution. Unfortunately, nothing had been made smaller except its horsepower; the only way to negotiate steep driveways was to swap ends and strain upward in reverse.

Even though I experienced the decline of that car from inept to debilitated, I somehow

* French for "beetle."

became convinced that automobiles should cost less, use less gasoline, take up less space, be easier to park. And, in the nick of time, the Volkswagen Beetle migrated to America and made its way, like Daniel Boone, into Kentucky.

My oversized Dodge had developed an incurable disease that wafted carbon monoxide fumes into the interior. "I've got to replace it," I

told my friend Ralph. "I think I'll get one of those new little Beetle things."

He looked at me in alarm. "That's no replacement! What are you going to do if your family wants to take my family on a picnic?"

"We'll go in your station wagon," I told him.

There was a wait of several weeks on Beetles, it turned out, but I couldn't keep driving the deadly Dodge. The dealer solved the problem. "Here," he said, "take this used one for $1,500, and I'll buy it back for $1,500 when your new car comes in."

Fair enough, I decided, even though the temporary Beetle had been made for sale in France and had its own accent. On the way home, I tried out the turn signals, little arm things that lifted up from behind one door or the other. Exotic, I thought, fun.

I flipped one up grandly as I turned onto our street. It was a warm day, and I had the window open, as delighted with my toy as Dad had been when he drove that '38 Ford home. He hadn't told us he was trading in the Model A, but from the front porch swing we saw him beaming far down the road.

My son, Tony, who was five years old, was at the corner when I rounded it. He ran home alongside me, laughing so hard he was crying. The world of television had come to life, he told me later—it was a cartoon car with little cartoon flippers, and with my grinning head hanging out the window I looked just like Goofy.

I felt like Goofy a few weeks later, when I decided suddenly to make a left turn, signaled, felt a crunch, and sallied off into a field side by side with a real car. I couldn't blame the driver of the Buick; just as I'd made my move to turn, he'd made his move to pass, and even if he'd had high school French he wouldn't have translated that little cartoon flipper into "*Attention! Ce Beetle ci a l'intention de prendre à gauche!*"

—ROBERT CANZONERI

BUGS ON FILM

Jeroen van Erp, a die-hard Beetle enthusiast and avid website builder, has cobbled together a list, a rather obscure gathering, of movies in which Beetles have made an appearance. They may not have had the leading role, as in the wonderful *Herbie* series, but any Beetle person can't help but notice them.

ILLUSTRATION BY MIKE QUILLIN

American Graffiti Youngsters cruise the strip in Beetles.

And They Walked Away Characters race Beetle rods, crash, and then walk away unscathed.

Annie Hall Annie drives a Beetle throughout the movie.

Backbeat Contains late 1950s, maybe early 1960s convertibles

Beach Blanket Bingo Contains a Thing and a Buggy

The Big Fix Richard Dreyfuss drives a 1970 convertible.

Born in East LA Cheech Marin drives a pink convertible until he gets deported.

Boyz in the Hood Cuba Gooding, Jr. drives a red and blue custom Beetle.

Casper, Spirited Beginnings An orange convertible Super Beetle is driven by a teacher and used to get someone out of a tree.

Chances Are Robert Downey, Jr. drives a red convertible.

Dazed and Confused Contains numerous Beetles of various colors

The Dead Zone Christopher Walken's early Super Beetle gets run over by a petrol tanker.

Dirty Harry A nice shot of a red and white Combi, and a Beetle gets run off the road by a bus

The Dying Fields Alex and his gang run a Beetle off the road on a midnight drive.

Footloose The roof of a yellow convertible is used as a dance floor for Kevin Bacon.

Friday the 13th, Parts 1 & 2 Contains a red convertible and a cream Beetle

Fried Green Tomatoes Contains a red convertible Beetle

Fritz the Cat A Beetle runs out of gas in the desert.

Gremlins I Billy drives a Beetle throughout the movie. At one point, steam rises from the engine when Billy's Bug breaks down.

Happy Gilmore A white 1970s Super Beetle slams into Adam Sandler.

Harold and Maude Harold's date drives a 1960s Beetle, and a priest loans Maude a 1968 Beetle.

Higher Learning The riotous crowd flips over a light blue Beetle.

Highway to Hell Various Beetles racing towards hell

The Italian Job Several Beetles in a traffic jam, just before the mini chase sequence.

It's a Mad Mad Mad Mad World Mickey Rooney drives a 1962 or 1963 red convertible.

The Jerk Steve Martin gets dropped off by a Beetle in St. Louis. Another Beetle is used as a ramp for a motorcycle stunt.

Liar Liar A blue Beetle appears in the junkyard.

Major League Wesley Snipes drives a pink late 1960s Beetle with Rolls Royce grill and Porsche 911 hubcaps.

The Man with Two Brains Numerous Beetles parked in German streets

Mars Attacks Contains a pre-1973 Beetle

National Lampoon's European Vacation A late model Vert steals the show in a big chase scene.

Pulp Fiction A yellow Beetle appears parked on the side of the road near a junkyard.

River's Edge Crispin Glover drives a blue baja Bug.

The Rock As Sean Connery flees from the FBI, a Beetle with peace signs on it gets run over by a Hummer.

Romeo and Juliet Contains various Type 1s

The Saint Elizabeth Shue drives a late model yellow Beetle.

Scream Main character's friend drives a red Super Beetle.

Sleeper Woody Allen finds a Beetle in a cave 500 years in the future. Later he pushes it over a cliff.

Sleepers A Beetle appears in the background as the characters have a conversation in a baseball field.

Stand and Deliver Contains a stock Beetle restored with Mexican style.

Tin Men Richard Dreyfuss sees an early- to mid-1960s Beetle and decides that he can sell them.

The Truman Show Contains a yellow Beetle with a dent in the fender

Up in Smoke Tommy Chong drives a white Super Beetle with a Rolls Royce grill.

Vertigo Contains lots of Ovals

Willy Wonka and the Chocolate Factory Contains about ten Beetles

WANT A LIFT?

Tired of the usual events in women's bodybuilding, Jill Charboneau astounds the judges by lifting a 1962 Volkswagen Beetle into this moving truck. Charboneau came in second, beaten by a sixty-year-old spinster who lifted an El Camino.

Derek Simmons purchased a 1962 Bug in Wolfsburg, Germany, and later passed it on to his little brother Dana and his wife, Jill. The two were so concerned about protecting it in a move from Ithaca to Santa Barbara, they packed it *inside* the moving van.

—JILL CHARBONEAU
PHOTOS BY DEDE HATCH

A Few Satisfied Beetle Owners

Odds are that you'd find most of the rich and famous, the royal and revered, the popular and political figures of the last few decades among the millions of folks who have driven Beetles at some happy point in their personal automotive history. Perhaps you saw **Prince Philip, Duke of Edinburgh** fly the Turbulent, a small plane powered by a VW engine. **Paul Newman** tooled along Highway 1 in his Beetle. **Ted Kennedy** hit the campaign trail in a beetle supporting his brother Jack's (that's JFK to you) bid for the presidency. Just to hint at the diversity, here are few more celebrity sightings:

Belgium's King Baudouin
John Lennon
Martha Stewart
Calvin Trillin
Harrison Ford
Sally Jesse Raphael
Lyle Lovett
Larry Hagman
Bobby Rayhal
Arnold Schwartzenegger
Dr. Benjamin Spock
Princess Margaret
Dennis Rodman
Hollywood "Hulk" Hogan

ILLUSTRATION BY YOUNG YOON

CROSS-COUNTRY PLAYPEN

It was August 1960. We owned a 1957 VW with sunroof. We left the youngest of our three children with Grandma and headed to Florida for two weeks with three-and-half-year-old Joanne and two-year-old Bobby. The problem was how to keep them happy and occupied during the long drive. There were no seat belt laws in those days, so we came up with the simple idea of making a play area for the kids in the car.

All I did was remove the bottom and backrest of the rear seat. I left the battery and cross piece, which supports the seat bottom, and cut a pattern and then a plywood floor to fit on top. Next, I purchased a two-inch-thick piece of foam, cut it to shape, and my wife, Sally, sewed a cover for it. Instant playpen. The space below the board, normally reserved for a passenger's feet, worked as a toy storage bin.

The kids were quite content on the drive. They would bounce and roll around all day, and when they got tired, they just lay down with a blanket and pillow and napped.

Where did we put our luggage? I built a very large roof rack. In fact, I've been told that it's the largest roof rack ever seen on a Beetle in this half of the country. It consists of two steel cross channels and specially made extensions

with suction cups to attach to the roof's rounded shape. The rack itself was built from two-by-twos and an army surplus canvas covered the suitcases.

I still have the roof rack stored in my garage. It measures forty-two inches by fifty-four inches—it is so wide it hung beyond the sides of the Beetle's roof. The rack did cut our gas mileage from the usual twenty-eight to twenty-one miles per gallon, but the car always handled the weight, and the kids, pretty well.

—FLOYD BENZING

IT AIN'T MINE, BABE

It was a recalcitrant, gregarious, arbitrary car, my '63 Beetle. I had no end of fun with it, and no end of trouble, mechanically speaking, from the day I bought it. Strangely enough, the battery seemed always to fail. I learned to park it on a hill, or push it myself, then jump in and pop the clutch. I came to know too intimately things like front-end bushings and alternators. (It would be years and cars later before I would learn the joys of a working heater.) But this was my first car. It had a sunroof and a good AM radio. That was the summer the Fifth Dimension sang "Up Up and Away," (which became the theme song for my "little red balloon"—never told anybody that).

I was putting myself through school, though, and a year or so later I just couldn't afford the payments ($39 a month—almost as much as my rent!) and the constant repairs. I prepared to let my balloon go. My father has given me singular advice over the years, sometimes useful, sometimes not. "Find the vice that keeps you alive, and live it," will probably stay with me for the rest of my life; "Join the Navy to avoid the draft," was not helpful. On this occasion, the injunction to go to the buyer's bank with the buyer, and get his check cashed before turning over the title and keys, would prove especially sound. I did so. Whereupon, we parted company, this buyer and I, he planning to return early the next morning to pick up his car. I gave him the title and keys, and patted a fender good-bye.

The next day he knocked on my door while I was still asleep. Suspicions loomed. Had I tampered with the car in any way? Uh, no. Had I removed or replaced the battery for any reason? Um, wouldn't that be a felony? Look, I said, I'm an English major—I don't even know where the battery's located. And anyway, I'd had a brand-new one put in, precisely to make sure the car would start—it's one of the first things a prospective buyer notices, you know. His face shook almost

as if he were going to cry. Then why won't it start? he pouted. Well, funny you should ask.

I got dressed, and mainly out of curiosity, followed him to the car, which was parked on a hilly side street. Sure enough, the battery was dead. A variation of a Dylan song of the era went through my head: It ain't mine, babe. I explained to him what I usually did in such

circumstances, and that the car was parked, conveniently, on a nice little hill that would suffice: But it was the summer of '68, and I had long hair down past my shoulders. He wore a crew-cut and those mirror-reflective sunglasses the Secret Service affected for a time. I was the enemy; and though he couldn't prove it, I had probably done something to sabotage his car, so any suggestion of mine was suspect. The only solution was a jump-start.

I was about to leave when an old black man drove up, precariously drunk in a huge, battered old Buick. Suddenly, a story seemed about to unfold, so I settled back down on the curb to watch. The old man was a gem, a sweet, generous guy without an ounce of malice in him; he just sincerely wanted to help. I can still see the mirrored glasses of the new owner caught in the trap of his prejudice: If all old black men are malign, or drunk, or both, then it is very hard to say to the one standing in front of you, "Thank you, sir, but you are three sheets to the wind, and this is my car we're talking about!" Mirror Eyes protested feebly as the spry old gentleman, talking a bit too loudly, gesturing a tad too broadly, gently pushed him out of the way so he could maneuver the bigger car into position.

The Buick arched, swung, and smashed into the driver's side of the VW, twisting and compressing the entire length of the left side, bumper to bumper. The two of us watched in silence. The old man jumped out and his apology was profuse and sincere. My first car—my eye's apple, my red balloon—now resembled a cartoon car, crushed accordionlike, teetering against the curb. As I watched the Secret Service agent gingerly work his way in

from the passenger side, then wobble down the hill and pop the clutch, and putter off into Cincinnati's Summer of Love, I remembered gratefully my father's advice. Every once in a while, I realized, you should listen to your father, even if it is the summer of 1968.

—JAMES CUMMINS
ILLUSTRATION BY DAVID CROSLEY

Lunch

> ## Living Large.
>
> The first time I entered a Beetle, years ago, was as a passenger. My friend, the driver, noting my cramped discomfort explained that his car was not a living room like those big cars but instead an overcoat that you put on.
>
> —SEYMOUR CHWAST

DAVE THE JACK

On a fall day in 1970, my best friend Dave Barker and I decided to do a little back country exploration on a promising dirt road in the outskirts of Spokane, Washington.

Recent rain had left our route a bit muddy but our spirits remained bright. We wound our way up the steep road for a good ten miles until the trail leveled out. Suddenly, the rear of the Bug dropped to the ground. "Damn, we've got a flat," I thought, but then the sight of my back tire and wheel bouncing off into the woods forced me to reassess.

Upon removing the hubcap from the dislocated wheel, which was eventually found in nearby bushes, we saw that the cotter wheel that held the axle nut in place had shattered.

When we brought the fugitive orb back to the Bug, we discovered a bigger problem; we had to lift the car to put the wheel back on. Anyone who has changed a tire on a Bug will remember that the jack will only go into a little square hole under either side of the chassis. The requisite hole was presently buried under six inches of mud.

Luckily my buddy Dave was a star on our high school football team and in preparation for the gridiron, spent many hours in the weight room. How different was a rear bumper of a Bug from some of his universal gym weights? With a mighty heave-ho, he lifted up the rear of the Bug until I managed to slip the wheel back on the axle.

After tightening a few bolts, we were off again—but without the use of the floor brakes. The brake line had somehow been severed in the melée. The parking brake was the only means to make a stop. Nonetheless, Dave and I made our entire trip down the hill and safely home.

The Beetle's simplicity, a little ingenuity, and a strong back kept many a Bug driving down the road.

—TEXT AND ILLUSTRATION BY MAX GROVER

THERE'S JUST SOMETHING ABOUT BUGS

Robin's egg blue. That's the color I always wanted. One night I came home to find a pearly-white Bug with robin's egg blue swirly pinstripes waiting for me in the driveway. I was so glad to have wheels. Later, the Bug became much more to me.

Everyone admired my Bug, even Bug-hating, Ford-and-Chevy-truck-driving guys. It was nick-named "the Cowboy Bug" by a few high school friends; they thought the swirls looked like cowboy-style attire or something.

My love for the car was tempered by nothing, even the totally undependable gas gauge, not to mention the heater. More than once, I ran out of gas. Stalling on empty waiting in the drive-thru was memorable. The Bug's shortcomings I managed to get used to. Like how it notoriously shifted into the wrong gear—usually, third instead of fifth. The screeching and skidding of the engine sent chills up my spine, but nothing could change my love for that Bug. Not even the doors that just didn't want to stay closed; while I was driving, they'd fly open, and occasionally my friends would almost fall out. (Finally, I did break down and get seat belts.)

One time, with a Bugload of people in an empty parking lot, I cranked the wheel hard and drove in circles until we were all dizzy. No one told me that Bugs could tip so easily and balance on just two wheels. I was also not informed that the car would jolt forward and backward wildly by a continued pumping and releasing of the gas while driving at two miles an hour. During one of those jolts, we discovered I could drive without my keys in the ignition.

Nothing swayed my affection for the Cowboy Bug: not the doors that flew open, the lack of power steering, the push starts it always needed, the fingers and toes it could never heat. I would still be driving that Bug to this day had it not been stolen by evil Bug thieves. My Bug was part of me. Friends didn't just think of me. They thought of me and my Bug. Even now when I go back home and run into friends from high school, they still ask about the Cowboy Bug.

—TRACEY SONNEBORN
ILLUSTRATION BY JULIA SCHWERIN

PROM NIGHT BEETLE

Mothers have a way of ruining everything when you're sixteen and going to your high school prom. They worry about you dying in a drunken car crash. However, my school was less than a mile away and I seriously doubted we could get alcohol at the prom. Plus, I had promised to come home right after the dance. My safety, it seemed, was not an issue.

Had I only known about my date's Volkswagen, I wouldn't have been so certain. Tom pulled up in a rusty twelve-year-old orange Bug. It sputtered, it gasped, it huffed and puffed like a smoker in the last throes of emphysema.

I wasn't any more impressed with Tom's appearance. He was in a ratty old leather jacket. Why couldn't he have worn a white disco suit like John Travolta in *Saturday Night Fever?* It looked as though he hadn't washed his hair in weeks, and his face had broken out. I had a feeling it was going to be a bad night.

It was. He didn't want to dance and I didn't want to dance with him. I refused to line up with the other couples and have the corny photos taken under a giant wreath of red hearts. On the way home, my mother's prediction of dying in a car accident almost came true.

Going up the long dark hill from the school, Tom suddenly bent down underneath the dashboard.

"What are you doing?" I cried.

"It's nothing, really," he said, "just the accelerator is stuck."

"Stuck? The accelerator is stuck?"

"Yeah, it happens all the time."

"I think we're going to crash!" I said.

"Well, why don't you steer?" came the voice from beneath the dashboard.

Although I had never driven before, I grabbed the wheel and veered us away from the rapidly approaching lamppost.

"Can't you just apply the brakes?" I volunteered.

"They don't work when the accelerator is stuck like this" came the muffled reply.

I saw a red light at the top of the hill. "Red light!" I shouted. "What are we going to do?" I saw myself entombed in a crumpled heap of orange Bug less than a block from my house.

"There!" Tom cried exultantly, emerging from the dashboard depths. "It's fixed. Are you sure you don't want to go out for a drink? I have a fake ID."

"No thanks!" I replied, and with trembling steps, walked to the front porch, hoping he wouldn't try to kiss me. "Never ever again will I ride in a rotten old Beetle," I fumed as I fumbled with the key and escaped into the house.

"How was the prom?" Mother said from her usual perch in the kitchen.

"Wonderful," I said, and went upstairs to bed.

—ELEANOR HERMAN
ILLUSTRATION BY NATALIA UGODNIKOVA

8 UNMISTAKABLE THINGS ABOUT MY VW

1. Our farm cats loved sitting on the hood trying to keep warm. They never figured out that the back part of the car was the warm spot.
2. My orange 1972 Beetle sported dozens of little orange fuzzies—the cottonball-sized "people" with googly eyes and black feet that

stuck to the "huge" dashboard, all of which were gifts from friends.

3. As with all VWs, heat was not a given. On snowy, midwestern winter mornings, I had to don a snowmobile suit, three or four pairs of socks, boots, hats, and a couple of pairs of gloves before attempting to drive it to school or to my job.

4. That car earned money for me. I "rented" it to friends who needed a way to nearby towns. It was done on an honor system; when it finally returned, it would be filled with gas or the ashtray would have a few dollars in it.

(Something you couldn't do today, even in that same small Iowa farm town.)

5. Dad souped up the car with big tires in the back which were more popular with the guys in town than I was. It didn't drive well with those tires, but I did get looks coming down the street.

6. I often returned to the car to find it totally moved or parked backward in its parking space (this was usually compliments of the Milford High School football team or anyone who wanted to make me think I parked it that way myself). This usually happened in front of Jo & By's, the local bar and hangout. There were times I had to circle the block to find where they'd put my car. The local police were used to it; they'd just shake their heads at my complaints.

7. The sunroof was usually left opened so that people could drop notes into my car for me to find later.

8. The saddest "unmistakable" thing about my VW is that I don't have it anymore. I sold the car in 1978 to put a down payment on a mobile home—I would much rather have the VW.

—KATHLEEN S. HOERNIG
ILLUSTRATION BY RYAN DURNEY

Top Ten Beetle Books for Roadside Reading

In the search for quintessential Beetlemania, several literary curiosities surfaced. Now there is Gerald Locklin's book-length prose poem *The Case of the Missing Blue Volkswagen*, Jacques Poulin's novel *Volkswagen Blues*, and Julien Beck's song of revolution *Living in Volkswagen Buses*, begun while a teenager and ended with his death in 1985. But here are some that might have escaped your attention:

1 *The Girl on the Volkswagen Floor*
A murder mystery by William A. Clark.

2 *The Official Rules of Punch-Buggy*
Now you can referee fights in the backseat. By Ian Finlayson.

3 *Volkswagen Churches in a Cadillac World*
A manual for small church pastors. By Mike Kotrla.

4 *Still Life with Volkwagens*
A novel by the popular British author Geoff Nicholson.

5 *One Volkswagen, Two German Shepherds and Me*
A book of fiction by Inez E. Lawson.

6 *Is Your Volkswagen a Sexual Symbol?*
Author Jean Rosenbaum began this volume of popular pyschology (what does your choice of dogs, houses, cars, and so forth say about your personality) as a doctoral dissertation, eventually publishing it with Bantam Books. The short answer to the title: No.

7 *Parson Weems & Vachel Lindsay Rent a Volkswagen and Go Looking for Lamedvovnik #37; or, Travails in America Deserta*
By Jonathan Williams.

8 *The Shanghai Santana and Beyond*
Managing director of the Shanghai Volkswagen factory, Zhang Chang Mou, explained his ambitious plans for the future to Paul Woodward, by Zhang Chang Mou.

9 *Rattlesnakes in the Volkswagen*
A book on reptiles by Joan Elizabeth Axtell. Herpetology at its automotive best.

10 *What's next, Pizarro? Discovering Mexico, Central and South America by Volkswagen*
A travel guide by Raymond Dyches. Just in case your other car is in the shop.

Bonus: 11 Authentic Sound Effects, volume 4
Not a book at all, but the perfect background music for reading: An Elektra record, created and produced by Jac Holzman, that includes the sounds of the VW itself. Other sounds include an orchestra tuning-up, an airport control tower, bacon frying, sleigh with bells, and New Year's Eve in Times Square.

BABY-SITTING BEETLE

My parents used to have our neighbor Bill White baby-sit for me on occasion, and one of his best ways to keep me occupied was to let me play in his 1962 Beetle. I didn't do much in it except to turn just about every switch and knob in the car that I could get my little paws on—save the ignition switch, of course.

Thirty-plus years later, I'm still playing with Volkswagens. My first car was a 1960 Beetle, and I've owned it for fifteen years. It is the car I learned to drive in, and it's also my own two sons' favorite pastime. They love to play in the car. Summer months, they never ask, "Can we go out for ice cream?" No, it's always, "Can we take the Volkswagen out for ice cream?"

Here we go again.

—CRAIG MERROW

BORDER-JUMPING BUG

I once had a job teaching at the National University of Rwanda in Central Africa. I didn't own a car and I walked most everywhere. My friend Loic Soulabaille owned a car, a sky blue Volkswagen Bug. One fall day Loic asked me if I would like to take a holiday trip with him during the Christmas break.

"We'll take the car," Loic said. "We could make a big circle, go down to Bujumbura, then east across Tanzania to Dar es Salaam, north along the coast to Mombasa, and west to Nairobi."

"Then what?" I wondered aloud.

"What do you think?"

"Uganda?" I asked.

"Your State Department says no travel to Uganda for Americans, no?"

"Yeah, let's try it."

It was the last days of the Amin dictatorship. We strapped two extra tires to the roof of

the VW, put two twenty-gallon jerry cans of gasoline on the backseat and hid various currencies in different places throughout the little car. We bought the currencies from street vendors on the Zaire border and from Catholic missionaries who always had the cash of many countries on hand.

In mid-December, we set off. With the jerry cans and the gas in the tank, we could easily drive over a thousand miles without a fuel stop. And with the extra tires, we felt confident driving where there were no roads. One day we raced across a savanna at fifty kilometers an hour as an ostrich ran beside us. We drove to the base of Kilimanjaro and left the car as we hiked.

We drove on to the Indian Ocean, pulling the car right up onto the beach, stopping only when the small waves curled up against the Bug's bumper. South of Dar es Salaam, we spent a day and a night on a second beach. This one seemed vast and the ocean so infinite that it might swallow the VW forever. The shelf of sand was so long and shallow that one could walk nearly a kilometer out into the sea. The air was hot; the sand was hot. When we swam, we found that even the water was hot. We attached a tarp to the rain gutter of the Bug to make an awning for shade. At night, the moonlight seemed hot and we slept under the tarp.

Farther north in Kenya, we swam again in the Indian Ocean. This time, it was in the harbor at Mombasa. The water was cool but oily. It smelled of petroleum and things slowly turning into other things.

When we came to the Ugandan border via Kenya, we had the good luck to get stuck in a line of dark sedans carrying Soviet bureaucrats on official business. All those heavy somber cars and our bright blue Bug were stopped together for customs inspection, military inspection, police inspection. The Russians neither affirmed nor denied our presence. They said nothing to us. But the Ugandans were reluctant to mess with Soviet officials, and somehow allowed us to pass through with our more powerful brethren.

Twice the VW saved us. The first time was shortly after we entered Uganda. We came to a large town and stopped at a gas station that might once have suggested the glamour of progress. The fuel pump sat at an angle on a cement pad that looked as if it had been the victim of some equatorial version of a frost heave. The rubber fuel hose, which had formerly been black and flexible, was now gray, cracked, and stiff.

We asked the dour attendant to fill the VW's tank while we removed the jerry cans from the backseat. "Fill the spare cans, too, will ya?"

The man looked at us suspiciously but did as we asked. We heaved the newly refilled jerry cans onto the backseat and got in the car. Loic stuck a handful of Ugandan shillings out the window toward the man. "No, no," he said, shaking his head at us and wagging his finger vigorously to emphasize his no. He wanted Western money, dollars or pounds.

The man grabbed the edge of the VW's door and leaned in toward us, telling us again we must pay in hard currency. Loic refused, and pushing the man away from the window, he threw the shillings out as he slammed the Bug into first gear and sped, as best the little car could, away. The station attendant didn't even bend down to pick up the shillings. Instead, he

ran into the station's office and came back with a pistol which he began firing at us. Maybe he only meant to frighten us and was aiming at the sky. Though we never had any evidence, we assumed that the attendant picked up the shillings after we were gone.

Later, we passed the police station where so many Ugandans had been tortured by the agents of Idi Amin. The building was still and

silent. There, and throughout Uganda, I remember mostly absence. It was after Amin had chased out the Asian community. In the cities and towns, there was no food on the shelves. Restaurants had nothing to serve. The streets were empty. Even the villages had an air of abandonment. There was a whir of insects over the silence.

We drove northwest then southwest around the curve of the collapsing nation. At the Rwandan border, the road ran out. Just stopped. There was a swampy area and on the other side of this swamp, in Rwanda, the road started again. We had gotten out of the VW and stood staring, wondering how we'd get across.

After a few minutes, a group of men and boys appeared around us. They helped us to pile logs on the swampy earth in front of the VW. Then, we all shoved and heaved until we had the Bug up on what might best be described as a rather long raft. This was the second time the VW saved us; the first time by speed, the second by light weight.

With the continuing help of the group of strangers, we pulled a log from the back of the raft, dragged it through the mud and underbrush, and placed it in front of the Bug. When the log was pushed up against the raft, we rolled the VW forward to the point where it was about to fall off into the swamp. Repeating this act, we were able to get the VW across the swampy ground to where the road started again.

The men and boys who had helped, refused any compensation. They stood in a semicircle and we walked before them taking each man's hand in ours. It would be fairer to say that it was not the car that had saved us, but those strangers, citizens of neither Rwanda nor Uganda. When we drove away, those people who had helped us went on home to that country that lives outside the scope of nations.

Back in Butare, we pulled the spare tires off the VW, put the jerry cans in the shed behind Loic's house, shook out tarps and sleeping bags, and prepared to go back to our jobs at the National University. When the new term started, I again walked to school and just about every day I saw Loic zipping by in the Bug, a cloud of red dust flying behind him. He'd wave and motion for me to get in the car and usually I'd smile and shake my head no. "I enjoy the walk," I'd call to him. As he drove away, the VW would slowly fade into the shade of the eucalyptus trees that lined the road.

—DAVID ROMTVEDT

BOOPMOBILE

In the early 1980s, Jay Ellerbrook and I bought a 1968 Bug. Inspired by boredom one day, Jay penciled in on it, freehand, the outline of the sexy cartoon icon Betty Boop. He then painted it all in, including the headlight glass, which ended up dimming the headlights too much and had to be scrubbed off later.

I drove the Boopmobile for many years, forgetting how unusual she looked. People would stare in puzzlement, and then their faces would brighten with recognition. I could see the words silently form on their lips: "Betty Boop."

—RHONDA BRITTAN

Thar She Blows. The 1999 *Guinness Book of World Records* reports that the car with the highest mileage on record is "Old Faithful," a 1963 Beetle, owned by Albert Klein of Pasadena, California. His car clocked 1.6 million miles before it was totaled on March 19, 1997.

Since the odometer goes to only 99,999, let's assume that Mr. Klein's in-dash abacus was sporting sixteen love beads on that fateful day.

HOW TO IMPRESS A ZILLION GERMANS IN TEN MINUTES OR LESS

I turned on to Bugs in 1975 while stationed in Frankfurt, West Germany. I was about to get out of the army and had ordered a new Mercedes van, which I planned to convert into a camper, then take on an extended one-year vacation touring Europe.

I had sold my beloved white Volvo P1800S

"the Saint" coupe. While I was waiting for my van to be delivered, I looked for a cheap way to get around and found a 1952 split-window Bug poorly restored with a nonstock thirty-six-horsepower motor, for $250. It had been owned by a succession of GIs who kept modifying it, then passing it on to other GIs.

It had working semaphores, sixteen-inch tires, the original head liner, one leather door strap, the original seat cloth with plastic seat covers in great but dirty shape, a "crashbox" tranny (that's no-synchro), a locking shift lever, two open-door glove boxes, no radio, and—get this—mechanical brakes! What you put into them is what you got out for stopping power.

One day, I was assigned to go get some training movie tapes. Big old "heavy" reel-to-reel movie tapes. I was also instructed to retrieve a projector and a separate speaker box, serious army industrial-strength stuff in weight. I drove through downtown Frankfurt twenty to thirty klicks (or kms) to the warehouse and got the stuff. I then loaded it all into the backseat of my '52 split and headed back toward base.

In downtown Frankfurt, I promptly got stuck in traffic. While sitting there, I started to smell smoke. I looked around to see what might be on fire and quickly discovered it was me! There were two-foot-high flames coming from the backseat and the interior was rapidly filling with smoke (remember, I'm totally stuck in traffic with a zillion Germans watching me).

With the speed of Superman, I jumped out and ran around the car Chinese fire drill style (I was so glad I had practiced this on numerous occasions while in high school) and began pulling film out of the backseat, as well as the projector and separate speaker. All the while, I was beating back the flames with my official U.S. army field jacket. I can only imagine what the onlookers thought, as I did my impression of Smoky the Bear in mortal danger. The flames did subside rapidly, but only after I got the weight out.

The movie tapes had pushed the seat down causing the metal frame to cross the two battery terminals simultaneously, thus causing great heat to build up. First, it melted the plastic in the seat cover ends, then caused the insulation under the seats to catch fire and smoke furiously. Once I relieved the weight, the seats rose up and the current shut off. I pulled the seats out and inspected them. Finding no extensive damage, and being a newly trained automotive engineer, I put something nonmetal over the battery terminals and replaced the seat, the film, and the projector.

Then I went around the car and hopped in—the car started right up and I split the scene.

I never had a mechanical problem because of the fire, and since that time, I've remained an air-cooled man.

—MIKE "MIK" MIKULAN
ILLUSTRATION BY GRANT BARNHART

THE BUG AND I

Can anyone forget that first car? Mine was an ancient, clapped-out, secondhand VW Beetle, which once might have been a glossy mint-green. By the time I bought it—for $100 from a student—its paint job had a sickly white pallor. It was the shade of green that's left on one's skin by old copper.

At nineteen years old, I had been driving for five years, but not ambitiously, and I'd never handled a stick. Too terrified to shift, I stayed in second gear for a month. Every time I tried to shift up into third—which meant muscling the knob rough and fast through an exaggerated H—I heard digestive sounds I didn't think cars were supposed to make and I quickly lost my nerve. Yes, the engine did roar when I went over forty miles an hour in second gear, and noises from the rusty muffler added to the general ruckus, and, because the springs were all shot, it sounded like I was driving a busted dinette set.

The inside of the car was tattered, as if someone had been trying to claw his way out. Perhaps it was psychosensitive, and had been driven to hysteria by its owner's neuroses. I couldn't be sure. But I did love the freedom that car gave me, carrying me out to the countryside or into the arms of boyfriends. In time I found its percolating noises as comforting as a cup of coffee. I would have given it up for love, I suppose, but not for money.

Even so, it wasn't safe at high speeds. Once, when I took a turn a little too fast, the rear end swung out and the car spun around and bounced off a rock wall, coming to rest in the center of the highway. A pause as I realized I was alive, then all of the fenders

and doors dropped off the car in one loud clatter. Though alarming, that incident wouldn't have persuaded me to give up my beloved VW. The windows could be taped over; the fenders and doors could be strapped back on with rope. No, it was only when a friend borrowed the car and ran it without oil until the engine seized that I reluctantly parted with it. So it went the way of all metal, to that great junkyard in the sky of one's memories. Ah, the Beetles of yesteryear.

—DIANE ACKERMAN
ILLUSTRATION BY MARK MATTLIN

RANDY & SOPHIE COHEN'S FATHER-DAUGHTER OLD BEETLE–NEW BEETLE COMPARISON CHART

CATEGORY	RANDY, OLD BUG	SOPHIE, NEW BUG
Power	Slow leisurely drive up hill gives you time to enjoy scenery.	New Bug *is* scenery!
Engine Placement	In back, where it belongs.	In front, where it belongs.
Price	Surprisingly affordable.	It had to be.
It Puts Me in Mind of…	The spirit of the 1960s.	How old my dad is.
Highway Hellos	Other old Bug owners honk horns and wave as they pass.	They're trying to tell you your car is on fire.
Trunk	Tiny trunk teaches virtue of eliminating useless possessions.	Plenty of room for riding helmet, boots, spurs, crop, English saddle, and bridle.
Special Features	It floats!	It kicks ass.
Only Defect	Valves require frequent attention.	Too underpowered to tow trailer holding quarter horse named Roxy, which we really couldn't afford, and which could sleep in my room, if certain people weren't so picky.

Historical Connection	One good thing to come out of World War II.	Are you sure it wasn't the Civil War?
One Nice Thing About the Other Car	New VW does draw crowds of admirers.	Old VW does draw crowds of mechanics eager for work.
Maintenance	It does require some work, but that way only very dedicated people will own one.	(rolls eyes and snorts)
Fuel Efficiency	Gets great mileage.	I understand I can't have a horse because we live in New York, but why not a puppy?
Sound of Motor	Raspy whine keeps driver from dozing off, plowing into ditch, and bursting into flames. Result: tremendous hospital bill.	Pleasant hum inspires driver to pull victim from flaming wreck. Result: tremendous cash reward.
Emotional Connection	Makes me sentimental about my past.	Makes me excited about my future. Although it is so unfair that you have to be sixteen to get a learner's permit, when many kids would be great drivers at eleven.
Sci Fi	If it were shrunk to three inches long, it could make an attractive medallion hung from the neck of Mr. T.	If it were shrunk to three inches long, it could fly off a magazine ramp and jump the cat. Who's Mr. T?
Driving Experience That Best Embodies the Car	Zooming down a highway in the Rocky Mountains.	Zooming to get the old man the help he really needs.

WHERE CAN MY VOLKSWAGEN BE?

Is it possible to lose a car in a medium-size parking lot? I often laughed at car owners wandering around, keys dangling in hand, wearing dazed looks of disbelief. It was a cruel habit, but harmless unless you drove a Volkswagen.

Especially a red one.

The particular day I left my car in the shopping center parking lot, I even noted it was in the aisle facing the jewelry store. When my shopping was completed, I exited through the jewelry store, walked down the remembered parking aisle, and up to my red VW. My key ready.

I hadn't realized there were so many fingernail marks behind the door handle. And right there on the door—a nasty new scratch. That's the trouble with parking lots, I lamented to myself. Then my key wouldn't work. I glanced at the tires. They weren't whitewalls. *Oh no! This isn't my car.*

Wandering through in the next aisle, I relaxed slightly. There, at last, was my VW. I had walked down the wrong aisle, a stupid mistake. By the time I reached the car, my confidence was restored. My key still in hand, ready, but the driver's window was open, the door was unlocked; I was certain I had closed the windows and locked the doors . . . unless someone had broken in. *Forget it. I didn't lock the car, let it go at that.*

Sliding into a familiar bucket seat, I discovered that somehow the seat didn't feel quite right. I reached for the seat belt, and clawed thin air. *Someone had broken in, and that someone had stolen the radio too!*

Oh no. Not again. Not twice in the same day—in the same parking lot.

I jumped out. Panic was setting in now. There must have been other makes of automobiles surrounding me, but to my eyes, the parking lot became a sea of VWs. I made my way to another VW, praying it was mine. As

insane as it may sound, I began telling myself what to look for in my own car, and performed a mental check list. This VW seemed to comply. First of all, it was red. It had whitewall tires. The driver's door wasn't scratched, and it was locked. Most of all, my key fit.

When I told my husband, Dave, I think he laughed too much. After he could finally speak, he asked, "Why didn't you just check the license plates?" Typical male reaction. Male logic. He had a good laugh at my expense, but that's all right. I know something he doesn't know—a secret about feminine intuition: *A woman doesn't need to look at a license plate to recognize her own car.*

—MARTHA LARCHE LUSK

KEEP ON BUGGIN'

OUR RESIDENT MECHANIC EXPLAINS
by Gary of Gary's Driveway VW Repair

Q: Everyone says Beetles were easy to work on. But didn't you have to remove the engine for many otherwise simple repairs?

A: Generator and fan repairs required engine removal, as did work on the heads. Some repairs that could be done without pulling the engine were actually easier to do if you removed it.

The record for yanking out an engine by a two-person team with basic shop tools is just over five minutes. On a good day, I can do it alone in about twenty minutes. That's only a third of the hour charge, and, of course, another third if you want the engine put back in the car. Well, maybe a little longer because you have to use a little finesse to realign things neatly. Trying to pull a chewed-up Santana tape out of the stereo took me a lot longer!

The fuel used to power a Boeing 707 for an hour would drive a Beetle completely around the world two and a half times. Despite the fact that many Beetle owners did manage a cross-country venture at some point, it's unclear how many hours, days, months, and years it would take a Beetle to complete that dizzying round-the-world route.

But an airplane's fuel efficiency is nothing compared to the space program's needs, which coincided with the Beetle's heyday. Laurence Van Gelder, then of the New York *World-Telegram and Sun,* reported about Cape Kennedy's space program: "The first stage of the Titan engine can generate up to 430,000 pounds of thrust, or the equivalent thrust generated by 219,000 Volkswagens." That's more VWs—buses included—than parked at Woodstock.

ILLUSTRATION BY PAUL LINDHORST

MACK BEETLE

My brother was halfway through his senior year when he installed something called a "header" onto the engine of our old Volkswagen, Bud, a little white car with plenty of dents. I still don't know what a header is. As far as I could tell, its sole purpose was to increase the engine decibels by a power of ten.

After my brother went off to college, Bud was left to me. Hey, who was I to remove what Big Brother in his infinite wisdom had installed? When I pulled up to pick up the carpool, there was no need to honk. They could hear my roar approaching a block away. The ham in me enjoyed blustering into and out of the school parking lot sounding like a Mack Truck trying to climb a tree. I guess they let seniors get away with stuff like that. Early on, kids would rush to the window looking for a souped-up dragster tearing out with some rough, tough football hero and see only a humble Bug ambling down the road shuttling its driver to tennis team practice.

So it only sounded fast, but I adored that car, God rest its unnaturally loud but gentle soul.

—NEIL JOHNSON
ILLUSTRATION BY JOSHUA SHAW

PUTTERING AROUND

OUR RESIDENT MECHANIC EXPLAINS
by Gary of Gary's Driveway VW Repair

Q: Why did every single Bug have that putt-putt sound?

A: Beetle exhaust systems were comparatively short, but not simple. There were eight connections to make when installing a Beetle muffler. All had to be connected at the same time—like wrestling an octopus. As late as 1984, you could buy one by mail-order, made in Brazil, through the J. C. Whitney catalog. It would set you back all of thirteen bucks. It showed in the price and it showed in the workmanship.

Few Beetle owners could resist the Brazilian bargain and lots of thirteen-dollar mufflers took to the American road. Beetles got louder—so did their radios by necessity.

Beetles also started chirping. The chirping sound, which is different than putt-putting, comes from cheap tailpipes. You could pick up a tailpipe for all of a buck. Then, in a short time, the baffles inside would come loose, rattle around, and make that annoying chirp (as though your Beetle were being reincarnated as

a cricket in its next life). And soon enough, a car with cheap mufflers like that would usually move on to the next life.

Illustration by D. Kohler

89

Waterproof

THE SUMMER OF HOT BUG LOVE

My 1965 white Bug was fourteen when we first met. It had lain in state on blocks in my college adviser's yard for more than two years like a corpse that no one had the heart to bury. I stared into its Bug-eyed face, stroked its coarse, weather-beaten Georgia O'Keeffe brow, and promised to bring its seized engine back to life if in return I could just depend on it. The critter seemed sincere, so we had a deal.

I hired this tall, skinny, blond boyfriend of a fellow journalism student (have you noticed how all Bug engine jockeys seemed cut from the same cloth?) to quickly rebuild the engine, install new brakes, refit it with tires, and rub off a whole lot of rust (using up the last of my student loan monies for the semester in the process). The moon roof, which while opening did a terrific nails-down-the-chalkboard imitation, had leaked rather liberally during the Beetle's tenure as driveway sculpture. As a result, the seats were completely rotten and the floors rusted. I added classic inventive VW owner's designer touches, such as a Holiday Inn towel directly on top of the springs on the driver's side front seat and a cheap portable radio on the floorboard, and we were styling. It was cool, after all, to drive a rebuilt Bug (my English graduate student girlfriend thought it resounded with Good Karma).

Our first full summer was literally a bonding experience. In 1980, summer hit Dallas with a cast-iron skillet, producing the hottest temperatures on record with forty-two straight days of heat above a hundred degrees. Five days a week, my little Beetle and I would brave a forty-mile drive to work around two in the afternoon. About the time I was sticking solid to the stadium chair perched on the driver's seat beneath me (I had updated the interior), I would hear a plaintiff cough, sneeze, and then gasp from the engine behind me. For the next thirty minutes or so I would sit on the side of the road baking in a Bug shell while the engine cooled enough to restart.

I started building this broiling ritual into my daily routine, and even began looking forward to the sonic boom that passing eighteen-wheelers created in my Bug.

My Beetle's sunstroke significantly altered my fashion choices that summer as well. I took to driving to work in gym shorts and flip-flops, no shirt, work clothes blowing about in the backseat—moon roof open, windows open, perspiration flowing like Niagara Falls. Upon arriving at work, with work clothes in hand, I would slink into the back entrance of the newspaper where I was interning and do my best to wash down in a rear rest room.

I coddled, cuddled, and coaxed many fun times out of that humble little vehicle, but I unloaded it near the end of that summer, seduced by a used Datsun with a powerful AC unit. After all, there is cool and then there is cool.

—JOHN H. OSTDICK
ILLUSTRATION BY CHRISTY TERRY

I'D RECOGNIZE THAT SHAPE ANYWHERE

I was a Volkswagen Beetle enthusiast even as a toddler. My mom tells me that this obsession started before I could talk. Whenever I saw a Beetle, I would point and make an excited noise. Whether it was the unmistakable shape or the putt-putt sound that triggered my response isn't clear, but my interest has never waned.

Once, at Easter, I received a chocolate Bug. My folks always created scavenger hunts with rhyming riddles for my brother and me to find our Easter treats. After a series of clues, I found it in the shower: a chocolate Volkswagen. Now, I thought, I can have my Bug and eat it too! It came in a yellow box covered with psychedelic symbols and Volkswagen drawings. One side was "customized" with flames, the other side with peace symbols. Unfortunately, it didn't last long—being chocolate and all.

I found another Bug in Austria, where I spent time as an exchange student. Outside a tile shop, in a village called Pirka, a car had been parked and covered entirely with pieces of colored ceramic tile—yellows, reds, greens, golds (Beetle colors!)—and then grouted. The Beetle must have weighed at least twice the weight of a regular Bug. Not a bad advertisement for a tile shop, I thought.

Currently, I'm a new owner of a dark blue-purple 1968 Beetle. I have no immediate plans to cover it in either chocolate or tile.

—AARON RIDINGER

Volkswagen

I heard that un-engine in front
not caring all the way up the mountain,
like your love letters not in
my suitcase when I left home for college.

Listen, the war is behind us,
and men have invented a car for
all, with a place in front where
we might still put love letters.

—**WILLIAM STAFFORD**

REAR WINDOW

OUR RESIDENT MECHANIC EXPLAINS
by Gary of Gary's Driveway VW Repair

Q: Some Beetles had a button for a rear window defroster and it seemed to do the job for a few months, but then, mysteriously, the system showed no sign of life. How come?

A: In 1969, VW added a rear window defogger, which basically sent an electrical charge across the rear window via a highly conductive paint. Scraping ice off the window did no harm at all, so mechanics were puzzled when the defogger consistently quit.

But from the inside, where the paint could be disturbed, drivers often shorted the little circuit by applying and removing Grateful Dead stickers and college logos. Typically, when a kid came home from college for the summer, the defroster took a hit as the rainbows and the skull graphics were peeled off so the folks would renew the insurance.

When I was in East Africa, the local name for Volkswagens was "Save the
engine—kill the driver." I've always stayed out of them whenever possible, and the one time I
had to drive one, I did not succumb to the charm of being in a kiddie car on a road with real
cars—and trucks.

I tried on the new Beetle (said not to be a death trap like the original Hitler-project car) and
found it to be extremely roomy and easy for a fat man to step in and out of. If I become less
flexible, and shaped more like a lightbulb (which is likely), I might consider owning one—but I
am *not* putting a daisy in the plastic bud vase, and flower decals on the exterior are not to be.

—DANIEL PINKWATER
ILLUSTRATION BY DAVID CATROW

HIGH IN THE MID-SEVENTIES

If you took all the VW Beetles that were on the road from the mid-sixties to the mid-seventies, and parallel-parked them end to end, you might get high on the residual pot smoke lurking in those vinyl interiors of iniquity. I don't know the ratio of straight Bugs to turned-on Bugs during that period, but the sheer tonnage of marijuana consumed in mine . . . okay, I admit: This particular red '65 Beetle didn't even belong to me. It feels proprietary in memory only because I spent so much of my adolescence as a stoned passenger in it. It belonged to my friend Mickey.

He was a good driver, and although I don't encourage others to wander down this wayward path, Mickey was unquestionably an even better driver once the cannabis kicked in. He became acutely observant, attuned to the flow of traffic, less annoyed by me, and more appreciative of the fine German engineering at his fingertips. It was Mickey's car. But the Bug and I were one.

We were one on the way to Truman High School, and one on the way home. We were one at lunch, when the morning buzz needed an early-afternoon boost, and one again in the evening, cruising Independence, Missouri's Noland Road, a main drag once listed in *Esquire* magazine as one of the ten ugliest streets in America. (Whoever compiled the list didn't gaze through a dense enough dope fume to see beauty in that eerie, four-lane mile of neon-fast-food-car-lot-strip-mall squalor.) The Bug and I were one with it, too.

Any pothead who ever rode in a Bug from this era may attest to its several handy dope-smoking features:

1. Wing windows. These have been phased out in today's less smoker-friendly vehicles, but for flicking ashes or emptying the bowl of a pipe without it all blowing back into the car,

and for fine-tuning ventilation without all that unwashed, uncombed, shoulder-length hair whipping your face, you can't beat 'em.

2. Decent radio (ours, anyway, had outstanding reception).

3. Great traction in rain and snow—and if you do get stuck in a mud hole or snowdrift, it's relatively easy to push a Bug out of trouble. Even if you're weak from uncontrollable laughter.

4. Visibility good enough to assuage or confirm a paranoid's fears.

5. Secret stash compartment. Stash compartment? Perhaps some shotgun passengers have ridden unaware of the contraband-storage cranny beneath their feet. You'd think Volkswagen's designers had held, oxymoronically, a stoner focus group. Pull the carpet away from that slanting floorboard under the dash, and you'll find that the floorboard is actually a Secret Panel. Remove the Secret Panel, and voilà—there's your eight-ounce Planter's mixed nuts can. Remove the yellow plastic lid from the can, and there's your bag of grass, your papers, pipe, matches, all the makings of the rose-colored-eyeball illusion and sensory-enhanced goofiness you seek.

I haven't smoked pot since the mid-eighties. I don't miss it. I do miss, every so often, the anything-can-happen, red-Volkswagen intensity of the early- to mid-seventies. Many of the friendships I found then have lasted, and my fellow ex-dope fiends agree with me that we long ago killed off all the brain cells that got pleasure from drugs. I rang Mickey up recently to say that my wife had test-driven one of the new Beetles and that I was along for the ride. It's a better car in many respects, I told him, but a bud vase is no substitute for a secret stash compartment. I'd have no stash to hide in it anyway, but it was still the first thing I looked for.

—JIM HOWARD
ILLUSTRATION BY WALTER KING

Sun Roof

PUNCH BUGGY

"Mom, are we there yet?" is the typical refrain on long car trips.

"Make up a game, and you'll get there sooner" was the typical response in our family. So our version of Beetle, Beetle! was born on a tedious drive to the Jersey shore in the late 1960s.

My sister Eleanor and I had always been fascinated with the colorful Bug cars, and we each tried to be the first to spot one.

"Beetle!" she would cry, gesturing to a green one.

"Beetle!" I would reply, pointing out an orange one. This quickly evolved into a game of vying to be the first to spot a Beetle.

I didn't always see the Bugs Eleanor saw. I am not exactly accusing her of cheating. "It was speeding by so fast you must have blinked and missed it," she'd say.

"I see a Beetle!" probably became just as annoying as "Mom, are we there yet?"

Our folks had to be at least a little happy that we never took up the other version, Punch Beetle, or Punch Buggy, where the first person who sees and calls out the Beetle's color gets to punch the other person in the arm. *"Punch Buggy, yellow! No punch back!"* Small consolation.

—CHRISTINE HERMAN-SMITH
ILLUSTRATION BY JEREMY SCOTT

WATER BUG

Charlie was a contradiction of terms. He was six foot two, built like a linebacker for the Chicago Bears, and took ballet. He was a high school wrestler who could quote lines from *Don Quixote*. He was my friend and he owned a VW Bug. Having a Bug and being my friend was not contradictory, but I was only five foot eight, and I drove a big Chrysler. I was from the country and Charlie was a city boy, but we always had good times together.

One rainy fall evening in Indiana, I learned that Charlie's Beetle could swim. Charlie came out to my house and we decided it was a good night for a stromboli run. The rain had been coming down for most of the day, and the country roads were lousy with standing water. Between my house and Kokomo there was a long slow curve that always held water on the low side. On the way to town, we approached the curve on the high side, and I warned Charlie, "Watch for the water on this turn, it can be deep."

"That's okay," he said, "my Bug can swim."

"Cars don't swim," I said.

"Bugs do," he said. "Some tests they did show a VW Bug stays afloat longer than any other car on the market."

I wasn't sure how this fact related to the long puddle we were about to hit, but I knew the water wasn't too deep yet, so I stayed quiet. As we started into the curve, Charlie accelerated a little, then straightened out just as we hit the water. The spray whooshed over the top of the car.

"Look at the rooster tail behind us," Charlie crowed with a grin. As we came out of the twenty yards of water we laughed. Charlie patted the dash and said, "Good boy."

Our lane was on the low side of the curve on the way back, and thanks to all the rain, there was a lot more water. Charlie wasn't fazed. "Let's see how high we can get the rooster tail this time," he said.

He swung the curve a little wider, straightened out a little earlier, and then accelerated more than before.

As soon as we hit the water I knew we were in trouble. The first hint was when the front wheels left the pavement and stayed on top of the water. They were quickly followed by the rear wheels doing the same. Then the Bug started a slow rotation to the left. Charlie knew what to do. He calmly turned the steering wheel to the left, but we continued to rotate. He turned the wheel to the right, but by this time we were going backward across the water. Between a

few well-chosen expletives, he spun the steering wheel back to the left with no effect whatsoever on the spin.

We were running out of water.

I don't know if I should attribute what happened next to German engineering, or to our overworked guardian angels, but as we approached the pavement, the Bug's front wheels happened to be facing the right direction. We had also lost enough speed so that the back wheels sank into the water, causing the rear of the car to drag into place behind as the front wheels hit the road again.

Our hearts in our throats, we rolled away from the water, pulled over to the side of the road, and stopped. Without a word, we both climbed out of the Bug and looked back at the water. It was about four feet deep and thirty yards across.

"Charlie," I said, "this thing not only swims, it can water-ski."

—DENNIS L. DOWNEY
ILLUSTRATION BY MIKE QUILLIN

Just Married. The only new car I ever bought was a 1962 VW Bug for $1,800 in 1963, just before Jody and I were married. We could fit everything we owned into it when we left for graduate school and our honeymoon. Thirty-six years later, $1,800 would get you a Chevy Lumina with 97,000 miles on it that a life insurance salesman died in after running out of gas in the desert.

And Jody and I'd be lucky to fit all our underwear and socks into a Bug, let alone the exercise bike and vitamin supplements.

—HOWARD MOHR

HEAT OF THE BEET'

OUR RESIDENT MECHANIC EXPLAINS

by Gary of Gary's Driveway VW Repair

Q: Once and for all, what's the deal with VW heaters? I mean, the manual says they have them.

A: OK, deep breath. Ready? Beetle engines warm up quickly because there is no water jacket to heat up—you know, the container that surrounds other engines and holds water there to keep things cool. And you don't have to worry about changing coolant or broken hoses since there's no coolant or hoses. But conventional water-coolant systems have one other function: They're also hot-air exchangers. Air forced through a miniature radiator under the dash provides lots of clean hot air once the water-cooled car has warmed up. After all, people like being warm in their cars. I can't blame them.

The Beetle engineers had to tap heat from the engine itself because the motor was air- not water-cooled. Theoretically, it worked this way: Fresh air drawn from the engine compartment by the engine-cooling fan is forced through a complex system of ducts and cable-controlled flaps, and, finally, it's blown out of various vents in the passenger compartment.

The first bit of ducting is the heat exchange box, which surrounds the sealed exhaust pipes. Then, it travels to the backseat, where it may exit or split off to the sealed and rust-free channel behind the rocker panel. Four feet later, whatever's left of that heat, emerges by the vent below the door, or the driver can redirect it toward the windshield by toggling a switch above the knee. This is the theory.

But here's what my customers have said over the years:

1. It just burns my foot.
2. I think since you're my mechanic, you turn it on and off.
3. None of the levers seems to do anything.
4. Heat? You must be thinking of some other car.
5. It comes out fine under the backseat, so I take turns holding my hands behind my back.
6. It works great but it's so noxious that I have to open the window.
7. It's anemic in winter and like a blast furnace in summer. (I can't shut it off.)
8. Fifteen minutes after I flip the lever for defrost, the tape deck thaws and begins to play.

If I duck, I can see out of a clear spot below the steering wheel.

9. I call it HOA (heat on arrival). It comes on just as I pull into the driveway.

Illustration © by Glenn Bernhardt

"DON'T YOU KNOW BETTER THAN TO SLAM THE DOOR WITHOUT FIRST OPENING A WINDOW?"

My Bug's Bugs.

Back in the mid-sixties I had a used Bug which, ironically enough, had a lot of bugs: Incidental features, like the wipers and the heater, performed so grudgingly as to be counterproductive, like service personnel in communist countries. I think the heater just recirculated the body heat of passengers. But *mein gott* the core of the car was reliable. I'm glad I never hit a deer with it (though maybe it was built so as to catch a deer at the ankles and flip it up and over) or drove it too close to one of those mosquito zappers, but it always started and always ran, and that's what I value in a car. Also, it cost me somewhere in the mid-three figures to buy and it never really burned any gas at all to speak of. In fact, judging by the heater's performance, I'm not sure it got the gas warm.

—ROY BLOUNT, JR.

A TEST OF VW POWER

The custody agreement in my parents' divorce granted us visitation with our father every Saturday morning. Most of the time we spent in the woods. What got us there was a mutual love for nature—and my father's red '68 Beetle.

The Bug held many mysteries for me, for instance, the true purpose of the "test" button in the center of the dash, which my father had labeled "Panic Button." When pressed, it lit up. Period. I fancied that it gave the car added power, or the ability to jump hazards in the road. On one particular occasion, the glowing button could have proved useful.

Following a steady, soaking overnight rainfall, my father and I attempted to drive up a rutted, muddy one-lane road to our favorite trailhead. The going was slow; parts of the road had washed out. My heart sank when I saw a four-wheel-drive vehicle stranded partway up the hill, two wheels on the road, two in a ditch. Mud covered the wheel wells and buried the axles.

Imagine my delight as our little Bug chugged steadily past. I was ready to press the Panic Button . . . but no need.

—KEITH ALAN FLINT
ILLUSTRATION BY RICHARD FAUST

THE HEAD
OF THE CLASS

OUR RESIDENT MECHANIC EXPLAINS
by Gary of Gary's Driveway VW Repair

Q: Wasn't the Beetle, for being so inexpensive and all, a pretty advanced machine?

A: The Beetle had a lot of features that were ahead of the times. It also had some stuff that was plain weird. These are some of the Beetle's then-advanced features, all of which we take for granted now.

- Bugs had shoulder belts before most American cars.
- High-backed seats with headrests showed up way before their American counterparts. (This had nothing to do with helping to keep a stoned driver from nodding off.)
- A dual, independent brake system was present well before folks in the government mandated them. That is, wheels diagonal to one another have separate hydraulic systems. If one brake leaks, you still have the other side's braking power.

- An electronic flasher unit made the turn signals flicker at a steady rate.
- The Beetle featured seats that went back—all the way back—as well as forward so you could pretend it was cool to spend the night in your Beetle on a cross-country trip.
- It had rear vent windows—pure class.
- Plus one key for both the door and the ignition! Who would have thought?

MEET THE **BEETLES!**
The First Wave of Germany's Phenomenal Automobile

Illustration © by Paxton Frombaugh

OUR OWN HERBIE, THE LOVE BUG

More than 250 Herbies helped to create the five movies and the *Herbie, the Love Bug,* television series. What other car can make that statement?

In his early days as a race car, our Herbie clocked 112 miles an hour in the quarter mile! But now, a semi-retired race car, Herbie mostly does parades and birthday parties.

We have VW friends on every continent and all of them eventually learned about our passion for collecting. Gifts poured in. Herbie's accessories hail from Australia, New Zealand, Japan, Africa, Germany, France, Belgium, England, Italy, the Philippines—the list goes on. Some original Herbie parts from his movie days include a license plate (OFF857), door handles, window cranks, and several knobs. But our world-renowned accessories include:

A rare VW fly, old logo hood ornament

Vented windshield visor

Four-piece upper running board trim

Side window plastic defrosters

Rare empi trim

Dog house cooler

Stainless steel fire wall

Cocoa mats

VW St. Christopher badge

Empi glove box organizer

VW cigar lighter

VW parcel tray

VW tissue dispenser

Empi wheel spinner

Quick shifter

Left footrest

Left foot metal trim

Gas pedal cover

VW compass

Empi sprint star wheels

Empi bumper bars

Empi bumper bracers
Fox craft skirts
VW woody rack
Chrome spoiler
Pop-out windows
Chrome eyebrows
VW checkered bra
Vent shades
Running board trim
Hella horns
Fog light
Fender lights
Whitewall tires
Door latch covers
Antenna extension
Front hood organizer
VW mud flaps
Curb feelers
Locking gas cap

—JERRY JESS

Beetle Stuffing.

The sixties and seventies were filled with students at nearly every university and fraternity packing themselves into a Beetle. Even the unofficial records seem to have conflicting winners, but several "teams" of twenty appear to have been winners over the years.

Recently, *Motor Trend* reported renewed interest in this with the release of the new Beetle. In 1998, twenty-five sorority sisters at the University of California, Santa Barbara, crammed into the first Beetle that arrived at a local dealership. Meanwhile, up the coast in San Francisco, nineteen bankers from the Bank of America managed a similar feat.

Just for comparison's sake, in 1982, twenty-one Plymouth Young Wives stuffed themselves into a British Leyland Metro. And in 1984, in Jacksonville, Florida, forty-two Moss Bay majorettes squeezed into a Jaguar XJ6. (This would tend to emphasize the "ette" aspect of the baton-twirlers.)

Photo courtesy of VWoA

SOMETHING BLUE

We were married on March 17, 1973, in the middle of a freak snowstorm. The "something old" that day was my mother's lace handkerchief. The "something new" was the veil my new mother-in-law insisted I wear after she vetoed the all-too-groovy flowers in my hair. The "something borrowed" was Aunt Ruthie's cottage where we would spend a gray-colored-Ohio-sky honeymoon.

The gray days probably inspired us to leave our love nest and go into town to buy "something blue"—a brand-new baby blue Volkswagen Beetle, a car we would drive for the next fourteen years. It cost around $2,400, which we paid off in monthly installments along with college loans.

Our newly hatched adult lives seemed feathered with a sense of endless possibilities, and our VW became the perfect vehicle for a new life flight. Blissfully ignorant of so many things when we married in our very early twenties, we knew this car was a sound purchase. The Bug had the same solid qualities we wanted from our marriage, and, if necessary, it could float.

Little Blue, as we began calling the Bug, because it seemingly had a personality, was a car of mixed beauties and great allure for me especially. The true character of our much loved car, however, revealed itself during the blizzard of 1978 in Columbus, Ohio. I was driving home from work and the roads were as bad as I'd ever seen them. The freeway frozen tundra was devoid of life. My colleague Tonda had a yellow VW and I had Little Blue. We hopped into our reliable rides to forge the twenty-five-mile journey to our respective homes.

Baby Blue and the yellow Bug took to the ice like a young Katarina Witt. The wind blew, but we held steady. There was only one glitch: the nefarious defroster.

Both of us had to drive with our heads stuck

out the side window. Icicles formed on my head as if Katarina had been dragged facedown on the ice by a Zamboni. When I mercifully arrived home, the rash from the cold made me appear as though the rosy end of a baboon had been slapped onto my face.

The next year, we drove our baby blue Bug to the hospital when I was about to give birth to our child. At one time the Volkswagen company had a "Bonds for Babies Born in Beetles" program. Their motto was ". . . helping to prove there is always room for one more in a Volkswagen."

As I was in pain, and swollen to the size of a hot-air balloon wedged into a guitar case, my aim was not to earn a bond. The ridiculous image of sticking my legs out the window to give birth on an April evening of swirling storm clouds offered me no peace. What I did like about that ride was that my husband and I were so close in the car. We birthed inside the hospital—so instead of bonds, our bonus was a big bouncing baby boy.

We needed ample space to deliver our new boy home with all of the suddenly acquired accompanying loot. Faithful Little Blue remained docked as our old brown '64 Chevy made the voyage. Big Brown had as much space as the QE2, which barely accommodated our planters, bouquets, gifts, cards, overnight stuff, sitz bath, pamphlets, receiving blankets, and an assortment of medical necessities. Baby, mommy, daddy, and all the kit and caboodle steamed back to home port looking very much like a giant maternity parade float.

When our little boy was about eight, lack of heat, a rotting floor, and the iffy nature of the brakes began to wear on my husband's levelheaded sense of safety. It was time for Little Blue to move on. The husband remains to this day, and I remind him often of the possibilities for replacement should his own heating system begin to wane.

When I saw that the newly redesigned Volkswagen has a bud vase on the dash it made me smile. I know it is to commemorate the Flower Power era when the Bug was king, but I took it personally.

As a bride who wanted flowers in her hair but was denied, I'd like to think of that vase as a symbolic token grin and wink from our honeymoon buddy Little Blue. Or perhaps, it's a symbol of that night, twenty years ago, and the about-to-be-born baby—now a man—who Little Blue helped bring to be.

—PATRICIA WYNN BROWN
ILLUSTRATION BY JAMIE COULSON

FLIGHT OF THE BEETLE

My new baby blue standard Bug was everything a seventeen-year-old could want. I even read the owner's manual from cover to cover—not something the usual high school kid does, but after all, this car was the hard-earned money from years of bagging groceries.

One day, heading to Vero Beach, I was stuck behind an old flatbed truck whose load of papers was flying all over the road. As I passed the airborne debris, something was sucked down the air louver under the rear window and lodged itself in the fan. I didn't realize this at the time. All I knew was that my new Bug sounded like a bicycle with baseball cards playing a tune against the spokes. But louder. I quickly pulled off the road. Being new to air-cooled cars, I called the dealership. Not wanting to take any chances, they sent a wrecker to return it to the shop.

The team of dealership mechanics fired up the car. The sound was unbelievable. They'd never heard anything like it. They were stymied. Finally, the service manager stuck his hand behind the fan shroud and yanked free a big hunk of a magazine. I wouldn't lie about this: It was an old issue of *Hot VW's.*

Thankfully, this karmic coincidence (what if the culprit had been *Family Circle* or *Look* or *Mad?*), along with all our laughter, spared me not only further embarrassment, but also the charge for the wrecker and the repair.

—RON GOOD

ILLUSTRATION BY OLIVER BROTZGE

DREAMING OF WARMER PLACES

This is one of my long-dead blue Beetles (last rites 1979), which ran two years, twenty-five thousand miles, at a cost of $250 (to buy it). First car. Here, it is dreaming of warmer climes. (Note the one small scraped porthole in the windshield.)

—TEXT AND ILLUSTRATION BY ERIC HANSON

BLACK BEAUTY

I nervously fingered the envelope bearing the logo of the Midwestern Concours d'Élégance. Be calm, I thought to myself, no Volkswagens have ever been invited to this car show. When I opened the envelope, I exhaled deeply and entertained thoughts about uncorking some bubbly. It had finally happened. Black Beauty, our 1958 Beetle, had been accepted to the Concours show in Cincinnati on Father's Day. It may not seem like much of a victory to Porsche owners, but the Beetle had been unfairly snubbed by car shows for too long. After all, twenty million people didn't buy Bugs simply for the great gas mileage!

My wife, Marge, snickered, "You've been attending too many VW car shows. I knew it would finally get to you. Black Beauty up against a million-dollar Gull Wing classic-design Mercedes-Benz sports coupe? They'll wipe the playing field with Team VW."

"Hey, I like that," I shot back. "We'll refer to ourseves as Team VW—it'll drive the Mercedes crowd nuts!"

I arrived early for the show. A heavy dew covered the field, and other car owners were unloading their rare and exotic treasures from special trailers. I felt like a 100 to 1 shot at the Kentucky Derby who rode his horse to the track.

Two orange-shirted officials emerged to welcome me. "You're a little early, but spectator parking is over in the far field area."

"Whoa, folks," I quickly said, "this is the first of three entrants from Team VW." Several officials were summoned in short order. I

heard one of them say, "I hope this chap isn't pulling our leg. Did someone on the selection committee actually invite a Volkswagen?"

After a few nervous minutes, an official triumphantly raised an envelope and shouted,

"Found it. The Beetle's in. Get him processed and onto the field."

Things were looking up until I was forced into a parking spot between a Rolls Royce Silver Cloud II and a Daimler limousine. By noon, thousands of car freaks roamed the field that included rare Aston Martins and Dusenburgs.

Team VW munched on bratwurst while Mr. Rolls Royce next to me set up a fussy little tea service with red-and-white-checked tablecloth—and matching napkins.

Surprisingly, his reception was cold when we asked him for some Grey Poupon.

—W. W. FITZPATRICK

Groovy Kind of Town.

While the Beetle's popularity took off when rock 'n' roll began, it was the sixties counterculture, with its black-light posters, incense-burning head shops, and protesting long-haired hippies, that claimed the Beetle for its own. And the Volkswagen van, too. (Not all your friends could camp out at a Dead concert in a Beetle.)

And California seemed to take the lead with Haight-Ashbury in the public's stony—decidedly not stoned—eye, followed by the state's tamer mainstream. *Time* magazine once described Pasadena as "a gentle cultivated city populated by little old ladies who sit behind lace curtains and, according to legend, knit Volkswagens."

ILLUSTRATION BY CHRIS SEAMAN

THE MODEL

I was in the kitchen when Lizzie came in with a plastic ice scraper. She was excited. She'd been rummaging in a box of mementos. "Here," she said.

I took the ice scraper. "It's a little thing."

"It was my steady companion all through the eighties. In the winter, I mean. I mean, I *always* had ice on my windshield. We went everywhere together."

"You and the scraper?" I said.

"Me and my *car*. Oh," she said, her eyes going wide. "I think I know exactly where it is! Hold on." She ran back to her studio, leaving me with the scraper.

In a few minutes she returned with a picture, a painting she'd done, and held it up under her chin for me to see. "What do you think?" It was a VW Bug convertible with the top down. A white-haired lady, it looked like, sat behind the wheel under an open umbrella.

"It's colorful," I said. "Who's under the umbrella?"

"My dad."

"That's Chet?"

"Yep."

"Chet never had white hair."

"I know."

"Why the umbrella?"

"It might rain."

"Can he drive like that?"

"I wonder if he can?"

"You wonder?" I said.

"Uh-huh. Hey, but he can see the road under his feet. I could. There was a hole in the floor. Ask me if I wore a skirt very often."

"Did you?"

"It was chancy."

"How about a bathing suit?"

"Not in the winter! Talk about chill. I wore my ski underwear if I was going very far."

"How far was that?"

"Downtown. To work. Or anywhere, really." A glaze came over her.

"Chet never actually drove this car holding an open umbrella," I said.

"Of course not. The army had given him all the cold and wet he could ever want."

"What's he doing in the picture then?"

"I needed a model."

"How come you made him a white-haired lady?"

"I can't remember. Maybe I was projecting myself into the future. You know, growing into a nice eccentric old age with my Bug. I can't tell you how crazy I was about that car. I mean, I really can't. We had so much fun."

—GARY GILDNER

swiss army model

WINE, WOMEN, SONG—AND GASOLINE

Driving is an American rite of passage, and red-blooded youngsters don't feel their adolescence is successfully completed until they've "soloed" on four wheels. Even the most happily adjusted child gets a little stir-crazy as the big sixteenth birthday approaches. There doesn't need to be anything in their home lives to escape; there is just some not-quite-clearly-seen thing to which they are drawn. Or, at least that's how it was for me.

My first car was a white 1968 Volkswagen Beetle. It would go up the steepest western Pennsylvania hills in the frequent snowstorms of the early 1970s. It was an era before El Niño and global warming, when "Get That Gasoline" was a popular novelty AM radio song. The Beetle was the perfect vehicle for the time and place.

I spray-painted the rusting wheels blue. I didn't really care about speed or power or even looks, just freedom. To me, a car meant the unsupervised ability to careen head-on into adulthood. Wine, women, and song. Or at least Iron City Beer, one-sided platonic relationships, and a scratchy radio that only got the local station (they wouldn't play "Honky Tonk Women" because of questionable lyrics). Time to be a rebel! Out there in the dark was the great future, seductive, impressed by my refusal to heed stay-at-home weather warnings.

—TEXT AND ILLUSTRATION
BY STEWART MCKISSICK

LADYBUGGING

My dad wanted to be able to spot the '59 Bug immediately in any parking lot. So my dad, sister, little brother, and I took our light gray Beetle and gave it a gorgeous paint job. It had glossy black sides, fenders with red pinstriping, and a school bus yellow top with red polka dots. (The dots were the size of fifty-cent pieces because, in fact, we used half dollars to cut the dots out of four-inch-wide masking tape used to cover the car for painting!) It was truly a family project, and as long as we had the car, everyone in our town (Stillwater, Oklahoma) knew us.

—DIANE GIBSON

LEAF MEN

This is what we wear on weekends when we are pupating, and this is what we drive.

—TEXT AND ILLUSTRATION BY WILLIAM JOYCE

PHOTO BY NEIL JOHNSON

'HOOD
ORNAMENT

It may be wack to admit such a thing to this crowd, but I started it. I was the first rapper to wear the VW emblem on a neckchain. If I'd been down enough to polish my rapping skills at the same time I was shining my new wardrobe fixture, maybe I would've bagged the record contract that put the Beastie Boys out in front, especially that no-good stolen-emblem-stealing Mike D. I guess I was just too beat from the process of elimination. Not the process of eliminating that chrome emblem from one of your Beetles—actually, it was no sweat at all—but the process of choosing which ride could provide the phattest accessory for this homeboy's get-up. (If you knew that "wack" meant "stupid," you also know that homeys now say "round" when we mean "phat." But, then, calling the VW emblem "round" makes my intellectualizing and glamorizing seem a foregone conclusion.) Anyhow, I'll save the sour grapes for Montel or Ricki Lake.

The story to get today's studio audience whooping, however, is not how those medallions started disappearing from rides parked in New York City during the eighties, but how I personally discovered that some car designer had been stylin' right under our noses all these years. That VW emblem was too far beneath most noses for folks to see that it might look best directly under one, swinging on a fine, shiny chain.

Even my search started higher—slightly above eye-level. The first serious option was the bulldog on the Mack truck delivering flour to a bakery across from my old crib. Because the driver kept popping in and out of the truck, I had time to weigh the pros and cons. Sure, up close, that mack-daddy bulldog looks as nasty as he wants to be, but what happens when I start moving to the groove with him hanging from my neck? Not only was I looking at gold replacement teeth—very Old Skool before Old Skool was cool again—but anyone at a distance might think I had a chrome Pekinese jumping at my jugular, not exactly bad-ass, like swaggering down the sidewalk with a Rott or Pit tugging on a chain.

Contender Number Two pulled right up alongside me on the hood of a Mercedes. But the headlights' flash and horn's bleep persuaded me that its driver might be summoned while I was still trying on my new outfit. Remember, this was back during the three or four months when New Yorkers paid attention to car alarms, rather than ignoring the noise or, worse, jumping out of bed to run outside and beat the ride even more to shut it up.

In the same time it took car owners to learn to prop "No Radio" signs on the dashboard, I decided against dozens of other hood ornaments. I knew my posse would give me more grief than glory if I wore that million-dollar tooth fairy lifted from a Rolls in the Upper East 70s. At the other extreme, prying a Yugo emblem, I'd probably end up with its whole sorry hood—and breastplates hadn't made the grade since LaBelle gitchy-gitchy-ya-ya-da-da'ed.

No doubt you twice-bitten VW lovers (first by the Bug, then by vandals) wonder why I didn't just buy jewelry like your neighbor kid in the baggy pants. In the days before suburban malls dealt in gangsta-wear, if you wanted something flashy, automotive and not o.p.p., selection was weak. In one misguided moment, I found myself in a car-parts store, standing in an aisle between crown-shaped air fresheners and under-chassis neon, checking out license plate frames. You know the ones: with the heavy chain border. Well, Mister T's grandma might wear one as a locket, but hanging all that chain on a chain seemed like overkill to me. I wanted enough jazz to navigate Brooklyn, not traction to drive the Taconic Parkway in a blizzard.

After much soul- and curbside-searching, my fashion muse settled on the VW.

As I recall, it was blue, with out-of-state plates, double-parked. The choice was obvious. Lightweight, flat, symmetrical, and—yes, my brothers and sisters—round. Not to mention easy to swipe. Just ask the Beasties.

—M. C. BUGGIN'

Owning a Bug sometimes makes you do funny things.

I created this photo to satisfy an assignment for a photography class. I stuck the leaves on the car one by one using an Elmer's paste stick. A passerby stopped and asked my name. Assuming that I'd be an artistic success one day, she said she'd look out for my name.

We've all seen bugs on leaves before. What about leaves on a Bug?

—KEVIN DeGABRIEL

BUG JUICE

Born in the late fifties, a bowlegged, big-toothed boy, I missed all the fuss and fervor of the sixties. Even the ticky-tacky seventies nearly blew by before I finally had the scratch, and the need, to ante up for a Beetle of my own.

College the first time around lasted two weeks. A girlfriend still in high school, coupled with uncertain career plans, found me ducking out of the dorm—and all normal expectations. Home again, I tagged into a busboy existence that would have made my National Honor Society adviser cringe.

But the fabled Brown Derby restaurant was too far to bike to every day. Scanning the auto classifieds, my eye ticked down to the muddle of gray at the bottom of the page where every extra word is a dollar more subtracted from the price tag: "'69 Beetle. $350."

Freedom was just another word for dark blue, runs good. A ten-minute test drive, followed by a two-minute stop at the bank to tap out the meager tuition refund that had lingered for all of a week in my savings, and I drove away a VW-inner.

Even though it was speckled with orange polka dots (Cleveland didn't become the capital of the Rust Belt by stuffing ballot boxes), I still thought it was the finest thing to ever putt-putt down Abbey Road. That inimitable, hyperthyroid lawn mower sound spinning out from the backseat again and again as it climbed through the gears was music to my ears; good thing, since the radio was kaput.

Suddenly infused with protective parental instincts, I stopped en route home to pick up all the necessary provisions to keep my ride in fighting trim. Oil, oil filter, spark plugs, air filter, wiper fluid, antifreeze/coolant—a whole tune-up kit and caboodle.

My father scoffed when he saw me pull the Prestone from the bag. "You thirsty?" he asked, thus starting and ending his weekly communication. Not knowing what he meant by that, I chalked it up to yet another sign that he was not pleased by my presence around the homestead.

I searched and I searched for the radiator. Back by the engine, nestled in front, under the backseat (where I did find the gas filter), even under the chassis. Humbled, I drove back to the auto parts store. As tentative as a teenager buying his first condoms, I queried the desk clerk.

"Where? You mean it's not right there next to the engine? Jeez, they probably left it back in Berlin. Just kidding, kid. It don't have one." An owner's manual emerged from beneath the counter and slid across the scratched, grease-stained Formica. "You ought to put your refund on the anti-freeze against this."

There was more in store in terms of the care and feeding of my mean machine.

The right front tire had a slow leak, necessitating a daily stop at the gas station. The horn didn't work. I filled up the tank according to the odometer since the gas gauge didn't work. Plus there was the whole heat, or rather, nonheat issue. But nothing could dampen my enthusiasm for being able to pop open the door, take a deep breath of that slightly-baked plastic smell,

and turn the key in the ignition of a car that invariably started. That Bug was the only dependable anything in my life at that point, and I was grateful.

Everything grew gloomy. The sun never seemed to rise more than a few degrees above the horizon. Night school stunk. My girlfriend's Christmas gift to me that year was "You know, we really ought to see other people, just to make sure we're right for each other." Tearing lettuce and grating cheese in my newly promoted position of kitchen prep was officially biting it. It was time to change my life, and since all my funds were tied up in Herr car, it seemed unavoidable that the Bug had to go, or else I would forever stay.

Four months of body filler and elbow grease had given my ride a new look. A royal blue metal-flake paint wrapped the round fenders in a near-rapturous sheen. The inside was scrubbed and detailed—all that remained to do was grease the rails under the driver's seat to allow for fingertip readjustment. My ad in *Auto Trader's* hit the stands the following morning.

It was bright and damn cold the next day, too cold for the mercury to even rise up out of its comfy little reservoir at the bottom of the thermometer. A potential buyer called and wanted to come over at noon. When I went out to slide the seat back onto the guides, I discovered the snow from my boots the day before had refrozen around the gas pedal, locking it into a "go!"

The mechanic next door told me if I could get it into his heated barn, everything would thaw in time. So plunking down a five-gallon bucket in place of the seat, engine screaming, my little sister positioned at the top of our drive to stop any oncoming traffic, I climbed in, jammed the Bug into first, rocketed out of the drive (while hanging on to the steering wheel to stay upright), then fishtailed into the neighbor's driveway, braking almost immediately to stop from crashing into his barn. Somewhere in the midst of that noise and craziness and sublime grief for all attendant things in life at that time, I realized I'd probably never be happier driving than I was on that freezing cold morning perched atop a tall feed bucket, fogging up the inside of all the windows as the car raced to warmth and sanctuary and good-bye.

—RICHARD HUNT
ILLUSTRATION BY MIKE BOLEY

ART CAR BUGS

The Bug is one of the most popular cars to use as a "canvas" or "art car." It is inexpensive, and the shape is already kind of funky and wild, which seems to encourage artists to make it even wilder. Hundreds of VW Bugs have been recycled and transformed into beautiful and meaningful art.

Some favorites: The infamous "Lightmobile" by Eric Staller features ten thousand blinking lights and a computer inside that can manipulate twenty-three different flash patterns. Then there is "Rocky Road," on which Doug Flynn shows off his landscape groundcover options, a variety on each fender. Carolyn Stapleton wanted to show the world the amount of garbage she found on the beach and made an environmental statement with her "Litter Bug." And after twelve years of meticulous labor, Ron Dolce created his Taj Mahal on wheels, a stained-glass-and-marble-covered "Glass Quilt" that shimmers through traffic.

I have made two "art VWs" of my own. The first one, called "Oh My God!," was so named because of the typical reaction upon seeing it. A hodgepodge of memories, feelings, and knickknacks, the car began to take shape when I was sixteen and I designed it to be bright and colorful like a beach ball, and as loud. One button releases a cacophony of chicken coop noises. The car also features all sorts of springs, sirens, a spinning globe hood ornament, and a chalkboard on the back. It is an "assemblage" art car, put together over many years, with new additions still added.

The other Bug I've done is a conceptual piece called "Pico de Gallo" (Spanish for "salsa" or "hot sauce"). The idea was that the Bug was driven through a storm of music. The front of the car has a concentration of records, CDs, guitars, and maracas. All of these musical objects blow back across the car to the rear, where there is a working amplifier stereo system. There is a stage on top and a person can perform on the roof—ironically, it can't be me, since I don't play music!

The VW Bug encourages the public, as well as its driver to be free-spirited, different, sprightly, and fun. In the context of "art cars," the slogan, "You are what you drive" is all the more fitting.

—HARROD BLANK

—PHOTO BY STEVEN GRUBMAN

ALL I EVER WANTED

I've always named my cars, which has caused some of my friends to roll their eyes. (It could be worse, I remind them. At least I'm not naming my body parts.) The cars I had before Volkswagens took several weeks before I knew them well enough to find each a proper name. Mr. Bumble's name, though, came to me the day after I signed the bill of sale. It comes from an animated film made in 1941, *Hoppity Goes to Town*. Just as the character in the movie says of the human being, "She knew my name. She called me Mr. Bumble," so did I know the name of my beloved Bug. And he's a good deal like his namesake: not much of a sting and sweet as honey.

All I've ever wanted in life was a job with the post office, a yellow Volkswagen, and a dog named Sam. Even a person like David Berkowitz had all those things. I'll never forget the summer of 1977. Somehow they knew that the Son of Sam drove a yellow Volkswagen before they knew much else about him. So

during my teenage escapades that summer on Long Island, whenever we saw the appropriately colored Bug, Linda Rooney, who ran with our crowd, would shout in terror, "There goes a yellow Volkswagen. It could be the Son of Sam!" Fortunately, it never was.

Now that I have a yellow Bug of my own, I feel as if I've achieved a lifelong dream. The dog and the post office job notwithstanding, I still wish Linda Rooney could see me now.

—DOUGLAS TRAZZARE
ILLUSTRATION BY ANDREW LUDICK

IN THE HOT SEAT

OUR RESIDENT MECHANIC EXPLAINS
by Gary of Gary's Driveway VW Repair

Q: Didn't an inordinate number of Beetles catch fire?

A: Actually, there were an inordinant number of Beetles. All makes suffered fires. But, here's my hunch about flaming Beetles.

These cars were so easy to work on that lots of people did their own tune-ups. (I'm not going to grouse here about how these same folks could have had a professional do the job right—and for next to nothing—just by pulling into my driveway, where I didn't have much overhead.) The original clamps that hold the lines onto the fuel filter were not reusable. The filters were cheap enough—like fifty cents—and you could find them on display at auto parts stores, unboxed the way you find lighters today. But that didn't include the new clamps. Hardly anyone had the original clamps except the VW dealership, and they cost a hefty six bucks each. (I knew Jake the Clamp Guy, and was able to pick up the clamps pretty cheap.)

So many drivers would replace their fuel filters conscientiously (very good) but leave off the clamps (not good). Soon thereafter, the hoses loosened and leaked, and gas went everywhere, which resulted in fires (bad).

But the Beetle had a special contribution to this problem: When gas leaks in the engine compartment of a conventional car, the driver can smell it, because the odor wafts back in the driver's direction, into the car. In a Bug, with the engine behind the driver, there's no picking up on the warning smell until it's too late.

NO BACKSEAT DRIVERS HERE

All I really recall of our Bug was when Zack, our oldest son, was going to the senior prom. The VW had for years been missing, more or less, a backseat. And to look closely at the highway whizzing under you where once, on the passenger side, there had been a floorboard, could produce vertigo. Zack could do nothing about that flight-simulator effect. However, he was able to spare his date the fright by ensconcing her in a paisley mini couch that filled the backseat gap.

—PETER NEUMEYER

Body and Soul. I really loved my Beetle because it felt like an extension of my body. Which part, I'm not saying. This would have been during college, had I gone to college. Anyway, each time I drove up to San Francisco on Highway 1, the car blew off the road. Drove me insane.

—CYNTHIA HEIMEL

SPECIAL DELIVERY

My parents waited ten months for this car. They used to joke that it took longer to arrive than my little brother David. I was three years old in 1957 when this photo was taken on Easter Sunday. I was a bit cranky that day, as three-year olds tend to be when made to wait for something they desperately want. Climbing behind the steering wheel of the car again and "driving" was one of my favorite things. Since there was no room for me in the front or back seats, I got the plum spot right over the engine, in the luggage compartment. It was warm and scratchy and a bit stinky back there, but I loved it. That spot put me closer to the little Bug's "heart" and the tickety-tickety-tick of the engine was always comforting.

—LOIS GRACE

While the Beetle never really earned much of a living in the United States, other countries put the Bug to work. The Volkswagen has had official status as a taxi, delivery car, police car, and mail truck—to say nothing of its volunteer work as a draft horse, shuttle van, dune buggy, race car, overnight camper, and moving van.

MAKE YOURSELF UNCOMFORTABLE

From 1970 until 1972 I was in grad school and my then-boyfriend, Peter Goldring, designed

and constructed a chair out of old VW parts. The chair was a real conversation piece. Even the headlights worked! *Vogue* (or was it *Harper's Bazaar?*) pictured the chair in one of its "Trends" columns, along with a blurb about it and the fact that you, too, could own one—for $1,000, I believe.

I lived with Peter's original prototype (and Peter) in my apartment for those two years. Despite its graceful curves, carpeted seat and back, the chair was awful to sit in. It was also huge, difficult to move, and incapable of blending with any decor except that of a car dealership. The chair remained a one-of-a-kind piece.

After I received my degree, I broke up with Peter. As for the chair, it suffered the indignity of being consigned to the trash, though I believe someone retrieved it from the curbside where I left it! What do they say? Old Beetles die hard?

—CATHERINE LIPPERT

FLOATSWAGON

In 1939, Hitler converted the Volksburg VW plant to wartime production. The original prototype was modified to create the Kübelwagen, or "bucket car" (which was later revived and marketed as The Thing), as well as the Schwimmwagen, an amphibious car with four-wheel drive and a propeller on the rear of the car that allowed it to move through water and then onto the shore.

The cars imported years later to America could also float, unless, of course, the floorboards had rusted through or the side-vent windows lost their ability to seal.

Sports Illustrated performed a test of the Beetle's floating ability by using a crane to lower the car into Florida waters. It took twenty-nine minutes and twelve seconds to sink—slightly longer than it would take a group of six phys. ed. majors on spring break to down a Volkswagen-size keg of beer.

Dangerous Mobility. I always thought that people who drove VWs ought to wear lederhosen, because they were always showing off how mobile they were with that little car, weaving in and out of traffic. They're the kind of driver nowadays who'd be shot by people consumed with road rage.

—RUSSELL BAKER

ILLUSTRATION BY SHU-MIN TUNG KALDIS

Volkstote.

Did you ever compete in the "Volkstote," invented by students at Wayne State University in Detroit, Michigan? The object of the event is for any number of participants to carry a Beetle one hundred feet (no, not a whole football field's length, a third of it) and then have all the carriers jump inside the car and drive back to the starting point. Your team's time would have to be well under thirty seconds to commandeer the unofficial Volkstoting record.

All across the country, any gathering of burly youth seemed occasion enough to heave-ho an unsuspecting friend's Beetle from one place to another—say, turning the car backward in the driveway or stranding it inside a fenced-in yard.

ILLUSTRATION BY ERIC SAYLOR

FRANZ LIDZ'S BUGS IN SPORTS

It's been three decades since **Evel Knievel** went down in history—literally—trying to jump Idaho's Snake River canyon. Thousands of Evel worshippers had gathered on the crumbling rim to give the daredevil his due. Hundreds of thousands crowded arenas and theaters on the chance that he would splatter onto rocks two thousand five hundred feet below. No doubt many felt cheated when a parachute on Knievel's Sky-cycle deployed prematurely, and he wigwagged to a gentle landing on the river's edge. "Originally, I was going to start the stunt by sailing over fifteen VW Beetles," says Knievel, the words rising like a growl from the belly of a Harley hog. "But the Bug owners who lived around Snake River were worried I might make a premature landing, and I couldn't find enough junkers to make the stunt look impressive. So I simplified things and just jumped the canyon."

• • •

During his five-year reign as the top player in tennis, **John McEnroe** often acted as though he were number one on the courts by divine right. But toward the end of his career, he began to look instead like Louis XVI on the eve of Bastille Day. His favorite pastime became lecturing all who would listen on the unbearable pressures of being John McEnroe. He never accepted the quid pro quo of modern celebrity: You sacrifice your private life. "I couldn't believe the way the press reacted to me and Tatum O'Neal, who was then my wife," he recalls. "We were out one day tooling around Central Park in a friend's VW Bug when suddenly we were surrounded by tabloid paparazzi. I floored the sucker and left those photographers in the dust. The next week, me, Tatum, and the VW were on the cover of the *National Enquirer*."

• • •

The Minnesota Vikings' bus once got so snarled in traffic outside the Silverdome in Detroit that the team didn't arrive until after the scheduled kickoff. **Fran Tarkenton**, the Minnesota quarterback, had to do his warm-ups in the aisles. The bus driver was so distraught that he called out the window for help. "Hey, buddy," he shouted to the driver of the VW Bug in front of him, "I've got the Vikings here!"

"So what," yelled the motorist. "I've got the Lions and six."

• • •

Bam Bam Bigelow gave up bounty hunting in the mid-1980s after a fugitive in Mexico pumped a slug into his back. Though the bullet barely made a dent in Bam Bam's six-three, 390-pound frame, he decided to try a less dangerous occupation. He chose pro wrestling, where at least the seats are tied down to inhibit the fans from hurling them at you. Bam Bam's signature move is the Nuclear Splash. To create the Splash, Bam Bam slams his opponent to the mat to stun him, climbs up the ring post, and

then hurls his body at the prostrate victim. This usually has the proper chastening effect; Bam Bam is a fairly fearsome sight to see diving at you. He is not only large, but impressively decorated—his shaved head looks like the front end of a nitro-powered dragster. His pate is tattooed with a multicolored ball of fire; his arms are a catalogue of mythic and symbolic creatures: a hawk, a griffin, a black panther, a cobra, a VW Bug. "My mom drove one for years, and always kept the cut-glass dashboard vase from it to put in her later cars," Bam Bam explains. "I remember my dad giving long lectures on the difference between air-cooled engines (only Volkswagens) and water-cooled ones (everything else). So I always thought VWs were strange." Strange, indeed.

• • •

Ray Bourque is a creature of habit. Take the matter of his hair, which the great Boston Bruins defenseman wears in a style that might best be described as neo-hedgehog. Each individual lock seems to pick up UHF, VHF, and radio signals from distant galaxies. The only barber Bourque trusts to trim his tresses is a fellow named Michel at salon Le Scalp in his hometown, St. Laurent, Quebec. And he always sleeps with a lumpy, yellowing pillow that leaks foam rubber the way a torn feed bag spills oats. As an amateur on the road, Bourque used to stow the pillow in the trunk of the cherry red VW Beetle his dad gave him when he turned sixteen. "I like to squeeze that pillow in a headlock," Bourque says. "I'm not sure what became of that Bug, but I've still got the pillow. I can't sleep right unless I'm hugging it." He means the pillow, not the VW.

• • •

Kip Keino still has the long, lean look that made him an unmistakable presence on the track. The two-time Olympic gold medalist wears a blue blazer now, and there is a hint of gray in his hair, but he looks fit standing at the door of the main house on his Kazi Mingi farm in Kenya's western highlands. He moves with the familiar grace and contained power that you can see in films of his classic 1,500-meter run in the 1968 Mexico City Games. Keino is a mild, decent man with eyes that don't flinch at life. He and his wife, Phyllis, have been taking in orphans for all thirty-five years of their married life. They have provided a home for more than three hundred children. Fifty-six girls and eleven boys, aged one through twenty-three, now live at Kazi

Mingi. They come from all over Kenya and Uganda, representing at least half a dozen tribes, including the Boran, Kikuyu, Luo, Marakwet, and Meru. Kip and Phyllis drive some of the children to school every day in a couple of old VW beetles. They used to drive pickups, but Kip says, "They broke down and weren't as dependable as Bugs. We're on the road three times as long, but at least we get there."

• • •

"**Muhammad Ali** just loved to drive VW Beetles," says Gene Kilroy, his former business manager. "One day, he was behind the wheel and this big old truck cuts him off the road. Whoom! We end up in a ditch, and the truck keeps going. Muhammad pulls out, races up beside the truck and shouts, 'Learn to drive.' The trucker hears this and says, 'Pull over! I'll teach you a lesson.' Well, Ali pulls over, and the truck driver slams on his brakes and jumps out. He's a little guy, five feet four. He doesn't recognize Ali at first, and he's mad as hell. He says, 'You think I cut you off? You *cut me* off.' Ali says, 'How crazy can I be? I'm getting ready for a championship fight, and I—in a little VW—am gonna cut you off in a big truck to get squashed? You got to be crazy!' The guy says, 'Are you...?' Ali says, 'Yeah.' The guy says, 'Well, you all look alike.' So Ali says, 'Hey, mister, I know you don't want to fight me.' The guy says, 'You're right about that.' Ali says, 'Come on, I'll treat you to dinner.' So we go to a diner, and we sit down and have dinner. The guy says, 'You know, I'm a redneck. I'm one hundred percent redneck. I never cared for niggers, but I always liked you.' Ali laughs, and the guy says, 'I want you to do me a favor. I want you to call my little boy on the phone and tell him who you are, just to say he talked to you.' So Ali did, and the truck driver shook his hand and went on his way. And Ali won another fan. Truly the people's champ."

—FRANZ LIDZ

All Dressed up and Nowhere to Park.

The compactness of the VW gave me confidence when driving, and especially when parking. Driving larger cars (like station wagons) I felt the unease like that of wearing a vast overextended Marie Antoinette–style hoop skirt, with the constant risk of knocking vases off side tables.

—MARK O'DONNELL

THERE I AM IN MY '67 BEETLE, MY FIRST WHEELS. I'M MAKING LOVE NOT WAR NOT TRUSTING ANYONE OVER THIRTY AND, ABOVE ALL, DOING MY OWN THING. THE BEETLE, THE CUDDLY TRANSPORT OF THE WOODSTOCK GENERATION, TOOK US THROUGH THE AGE OF AQUARIUS AND, HONEST MOM, I NEVER INHALED.

THE CAR HOWEVER HAS ITS SINISTER ORIGIN IN HITLER'S REIGN AS A "PEOPLES CAR" FOR GERMANY. —————— NOW THE NEW BEETLE IS WITH US AND MAY ALL WHO DRIVE IT LIVE THROUGH INTERESTING TIMES.

—TEXT AND ILLUSTRATION BY STUART LEEDS

THINGS THAT FIT IN MY BIG BAD BUG

Why buy a Beetle? Aside from its price—$2,000—my legs would reach the foot controls easily, which was not always the case with American cars. And it was larger inside than it appeared. I once squeezed an entire family into it, three adults and several children, with one child scrunched onto the back window ledge. With the backseat down, I once wedged a full-size wheelbarrow inside. Once when I bought an apple tree, the nursery man placed it into the front luggage compartment, its branches sticking out. "Do you have another car to take this home in?" he asked. My Bug was big, but not that big. We squeezed it in, and I drove home, trying not to get too close and poke the cars ahead of me.

—JANET OVERMYER
ILLUSTRATION BY OLIVER BROTZGE

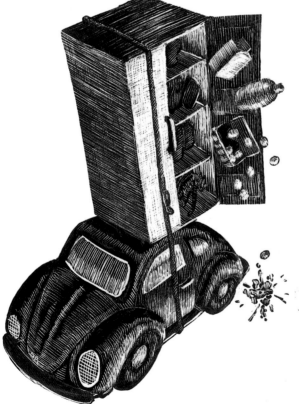

5 THINGS THAT
WON'T FIT

A CURIOSITY OF BEETLES

My father bought the first VW in this part of the country (South Georgia, North Florida) in the early fifties. I'm not sure when, but it seems like it was about the summer of 1953. I remember the car. It was exactly the same color as tomato soup. He bought it because our old cook kept wearing out the Ford station wagon that we provided as transportation back and forth over the muddy clay roads. Because the cook was indispensable and refused to move away from her own place way the hell down by the river, we had to do something. Somewhere, my father read that these cheap little rear-engined cars would pull through (actually push through) muddy roads just as well as a station wagon. By the time he had made the five-hour drive all the way from Jacksonville in the new little "Volkswagen," he was infatuated, and the cook wound up with the station wagon.

Two other VWs (blue and green) came almost immediately so that we children and our mother would quit driving off in "his car." When it rained and the roads got muddy, I had to go get the cook in the green one. She would say, "You ought to let me have this little bomb and you drive the station wagon. That way, you wouldn't have to come all the way down through all these bad roads to get me on wet-assed mornings like this. Besides, you ain't never going to get no girl in the backseat of this little thing—ain't no place to put your feet."

I would reply, "I ain't interested in that right now, I'm too young."

"Yeah, right," she would say. "You would do a heap better with a nice big white station wagon. You swap with me and I'll put in a good word for you down by the bridge."

"I didn't think it had anything to do with feet," I said.

We had variations of this same conversation on wet mornings for a long time.

Those VWs were a great curiosity around there and when one stopped, all the mechanics in the county came to examine it. Only the most intelligent of them could find where the motor was hidden. Most were perplexed.

"Hell, it got to have one, I can hear it running."

"Yeah, it's back here, look at them little tailpipes—that's where the exhaust is at. All you have to do is foller them and you will find the motor, stands to reason."

"Ain't a goddamn thing up under here but a buncha little pipes going every whichaway—whoo—hotter'n hell—sombitch must have thirty cylinders—all these little hot-assed pipes."

"Maybe if we opened this lid."

"We getting close. Here go the generator and a little distributor and a coil. You was wrong, ain't got but four cylinders."

"Yeah, I can see that but where the hell is they at? The spark plug wires just go through them little holes in that tin right down to the road. Ain't got no fan neither."

"Shit, this ain't no kinda real car. It was just made for the movies."

When I got married in 1961, I was in the navy and stationed in Puerto Rico. My mamma, as a joke maybe, sent me the old green Volkswagen for my wedding present. The navy shipped it way up in the bow of a carrier on the hangar deck. It was pretty rusty when it got there, but I was glad to see it. Since it was the fastest of the bunch, it had always been my favorite. My wife and I drove it all over Puerto Rico. Finally, the rust and those years of bad roads and irresponsible abuse caused a gas tank leak. I was always going to get around to fixing it—like I fixed the rotted-out sunroof (I think that was the first VW with a sunroof sold in the United States—1954, 1955? roller on the gas pedal style) by carrying a little boat on top all the time.

When the time came for my first son to be born, we were still pouring the gas in for each trip and catching it when it ran out in a dishpan under the car. We didn't even need a funnel to put it back in because the gas hole was so big. In the middle of putting my wife in the car, I stomped in the gas pan and (between contractions) we had to turn my motor scooter upside down for its gas. Everything worked out fine except they wouldn't let me stay in the waiting room because my foot smelled so strongly of gasoline.

When the time came to get out of the navy, I shipped the old rusted-out junk pile home and we drove it for years. I used an outboard motor gas tank in the "way back" to circumvent the leak. Finally the clutch cable rusted out irreparably, and we drove it without a clutch—cranked up in gear and changed gears by synchronizing with the throttle, like a tractor. A funny thing about the old green car though, ragged as it got, it was still the fastest.

One time, toward the end, I was coming back from New Orleans at two in the morning when the battery hopped off its little support board that I built. It fell through the rusty hole in the floor and was dragged to pieces down on the highway. At first, the lights went out and the engine cut off. Then, suddenly, everything got snatched completely loose, I guess, and the lights came back on, the old engine picked up, and we tooled it home on the generator.

My whole family drove Volkswagens until they got to be as high priced and silly as Edsels. Mamma even bought a Rabbit. It stayed tore up and in the shop all the time. Right about when the bumpers got square, the fun went out of it and most of us changed over to Japanese pickup trucks. Hell, I even reverted back to Ford station wagons.

The cook was wrong. There are plenty of places to put your feet in a VW.

—ROBB WHITE
ILLUSTRATION BY SHEILA TAWNEY

What Hit Me? A drunk is knocked down by a gallumphing St. Bernard, and then, staggering to his feet, he's hit by a passing Volkswagen Beetle. Bystanders rush over to help.

"I'm okay," the drunk replies. "The dog didn't hurt so much but that tin can tied to his tail nearly killed me!"

ILLUSTRATION BY KELLY SPARKS

149

VALERIE AND HER VOLKSWAGENS

When I was in my twenties, the VW Bug was a unit of measure first, and a mode of transportation second. I grew up in the sixties, an anti-materialistic son of the middle class. I wasn't against private property, I was against stuff. Books were okay and some clothing, but that was it. I didn't want my life cluttered with stuff. I knew that I'd never own more property than I could move in a VW Bug. When I headed for graduate school, I was sure I'd be leading a footloose life of travel and fast getaways. I didn't want to be encumbered.

Because I was against stuff, I didn't even have a car to move the few things I did own. Happily, my girlfriend did. Valerie's yellow VW dated from 1967. By the time we got to know each other in the early seventies, it had a hundred thousand miles on it. Together we added thousands more. She drove out to visit when I was working in northern California. We went to see her father in Baja, camping up and down the coast out of the front of her car. We drove back to Maine, then we moved me, my books, and typewriter to Chicago. During the long drives, Valerie listened patiently to my anxious rants about freedom and nonencumbrance and the soul-killing nature of academic life.

Although Valerie's background was more exotic than her VW's—her parents had been in the picture business in California; she had grown up in Mexico City—she and the VW were a good match. Valerie was practical, could take care of herself, and was good for the long haul. So was the VW. She was interesting-looking. People were drawn to her. Ditto the car. Moreover, she was at her best in trying circumstances (some of which involved a callow, often clueless boyfriend). In a blizzard late one December night, the car broke down while we were driving east. Valerie got out and went back to inspect the engine. The snow wasn't letting up and I wondered if we might not be camping in the backseat. Valerie handed me a flashlight, turned to a likely page in the repair manual, and told me to stay in the car and read the instructions to her step by step. In five minutes, we were on our way.

When things went wrong between us, it was more than a flashlight could fix. We stayed friends. She developed a passion for the Boston Red Sox, but the yellow VW had too many miles on it for her to feel safe driving to Winter Haven for spring training. She sold it to the teenager next door and bought herself a VW Rabbit, a diesel, and off she went. It was silver, had a sun-roof, a quartz clock, and a first-rate sound system. The Rabbit was shorter on style than the Beetle, but Valerie packed the new car as expertly and drove it as confidently as she had the old one. To me, it was just an avatar of her yellow VW.

Valerie liked to twit me about the young man I had been and my old horror of possessions. She threatened to leave me the Rabbit and two televisions in her will. Idle teasing, I thought; we would be driving to the baseball games in this VW or another one well into the twenty-first century. But I was mistaken. Valerie died.

The Rabbit was now mine. The moonshell from Florida stayed on the dashboard where she'd left it. Once in a while, I'd play her Willie Nelson tapes, and I kept track of gas mileage in the same silver-backed notebook she used. Every summer when it was warm enough, I'd crank back the sunroof, and remember what a sun lover she was. I meant to drive that car into the year 2000 and beyond, but Maine winters are hard on diesel Rabbits. It lasted ten more years.

When I replaced it with an ancient Volvo, the gardenia perfume, the moonshell, and the silver notebook were moved to its glove box. Metempsychosis is real; mementos make it visible.

—**WALLACE PINFOLD**

Death Be Not Proud.

In my twenties I bought a used VW Bug for $100. The owner said he just wanted to get rid of it. He looked pained, and couldn't guarantee it would even make it through the summer.

There was a problem with the oil. Apparently the car was either burning oil, leaking oil, or just perspiring a lot.

"I just want to get rid of it," he said, like a man who couldn't bear watching a close friend die.

So I bought it. I didn't really want to own a car, and this didn't look like it would be a car for long.

It lasted four years. Then, one day, it died. But I'd rather not talk about that. . . .

—**PAUL HELLMAN**

The Beat Goes On.
In 1962, having just completed the score for the *Manchurian Candidate*, I decided that I'd get a car to celebrate. I spent most of my share of the commission on a concert of my symphonic work at Town Hall in New York City. When the person helping me put on the concert ran out of money, I had to use my profits from the film to pay all the musicians I'd recruited. My girlfriend at the time said, "Here you wrote this wonderful film score for this wonderful film, you should get something for yourself."

I explained that the music was the best reward, but I did have about $1,600 left. I stumbled upon a VW Beetle that was a year old and in perfect condition. I thought a Beetle would be just the right size to fit my girlfriend, my French horn, and two suitcases. Since I was single, that's all I needed to drive anywhere.

I loved that car. Fun to drive, easy to park, and, at that time, a great conversation piece. What amazed me most was how every single inch of the car had been designed to take up as little room as possible, yet also afford as much room as possible. There wasn't anything in the car that was fancy, extra, or superfluous. As a composer, you try to say as much as possible without wasting a note. The Beetle was a car after my own heart.

Four years ago, I went to Tepoztlán, Mexico, to write an orchestral piece for a young people's symphony, and my host, Brooks Jones, offered me the use of his car. "Have you ever seen one of these?" he asked, and pointed out his Beetle—it was ten years old with at least 180,000 miles. My wife and I and our three kids all squeezed into it. We drove all around Tepoztlán and I recalled how in 1962 and 1963, playing music with Dizzy Gillespie, riding around with Jack Kerouac, and generally being a free spirit in my Beetle, I never dreamed that I'd have a family and that, one day, I'd be riding in a VW Beetle again.

—DAVID AMRAM

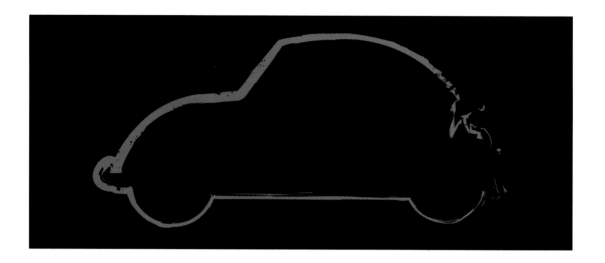

SWEET DREAMS

I owned a cherry-red 1966 Bug, complete with every quirk and character trait that epitomized a love/hate relationship. When I drove her, I felt oddly invincible, despite the fact that she was the smallest vehicle on the road. Passing a tractor trailer on a bridge in the wind guaranteed an adrenaline rush. She was unstoppable. Moreover, we took care of each other. I alternately cleaned, fixed, begged, cursed, and cajoled. In return she brought me home in one piece when I should have been broken more times than I care to remember.

Once on a long drive home in a snow-storm, I fell asleep at the wheel. I only remember waking up, suddenly alert, trembling, and shocked: How long had I been out? Yet I made it home safely, went to bed, and thought nothing more about it until the following day, when I noticed that both of the passenger-side fenders were flattened flush with the wheels, and that large splinters of bark were wedged under the hubcaps. To this day, despite having investigated, I never discovered just what tree, pole, or fence I had clipped, or how that car managed to keep us in one piece, with me asleep at the wheel. There's no explaining some relationships.

**—TEXT AND ILLUSTRATION
BY BILL SIENKIEWICZ**

FROM "A SNOB'S GUIDE TO STATUS CARS" 1964

If you're not married, take women who are college graduates to little theater or terribly smart cocktail parties or to a picnic in the country, but don't do anything with them until you're married and then, when you're married, make a slat bench and have at least three children and name them after characters from Winnie-the-Pooh. Take out your contact lenses before making love. Use a lot of Freudian terminology in your speech unless you have been through psychoanalysis. Go through psychoanalysis. Own the complete works of Copland or Vivaldi. Read the *New Yorker* and check off all the movies in the front of the magazine after you have seen them. Read *Time* but hate it. Spend a lot of time on your modest hi-fi and leave the components exposed. Enjoy Joan Baez. Tell people you voted for Stevenson the first time he ran but not the second. If you are Jewish and somebody should ask you what kind of a car you drive, say: "A VW, and I know, but it's a helluva solid little piece of machinery." Go to any Ingmar Bergman movie and correctly identify Max von Sydow and at least three other actors, telling what roles they played in *Wild Strawberries* and *Smiles of a Summer Night.* (If your Volkswagen is a Karmann Ghia, you should have been able to interpret *The Seventh Seal* on at least three levels.) It is all right to take a Volkswagen to a concert, to an indoor art exhibit, or to a university extension class. It is not all right to take a Volkswagen to a Great Book discussion or to a meeting of the Birch Society. If you have a small sticker on your back window that reads "made in der Black Forest by der elves," you should be driving a Metropolitan.

—DAN GREENBURG

ACKNOWLEDGMENTS

I'd like to extend my gratitude and credit many individuals for their advice and support during the creating of *My Bug.* First, I owe inestimable thanks to Jay Rishel who acted as project manager throughout the process, and to Mark Svede who managed most everything else. I'm especially appreciative of contributions by members of Columbus College of Art and Design—faculty members Walter King and Stewart McKissick, in particular—as well as the students and graduates who created artwork. Franz Lidz's interviews and Eric Hanson's illustrations both came as genuine gifts from sympathetic spirits, and I hope to be able to return such favors. Marc Cohen and his patient, generous stable of cartoonists deserve a special thanks as well. Once again, I'm indebted to Will Shively for lending his time and photographic skills.

I would also like to acknowledge the generosity of Mark Garrett and Marilyn Allen, of Central Ohio Vintage Volkswagen Club; and Ray Fortin of Autometrics, Inc.; Wallace Pinfold; Linda Hengst of the Ohioana Library; and the timely advice of my friends Max Rudin, Alice Siempelkamp, Sharon Reiss, and Common Gear VW newsletter (commongear@aol.com). My thanks to Mike Epstein and to Volkswagen of America for the use of their photographs.

Specified acknowledgment and appreciation is due for the use of these contributions:

Illustrations by Peter Aschwanden from *How to Keep Your Volkswagen Alive,* by John Muir, © John Muir Publications, Santa Fe. Reprinted with permission of Eve Muir. Enormous thanks to Peter for creating—and hand-lettering—his piece.

Photographs by Harrod Blank of particular customized Beetles are reprinted with thanks to the cars' creators: "Lightmobile," (created and photographed by Eric Staller); "Wrought-Iron VW," Joe Gomez; "Marble Madness," Ron Dolce.

Finally, my thanks to each of the contributors, illustrators, photographers, and writers for creating this legacy of Beetle lore, legend, and, let's admit it, lunacy.

CREDITS

PHOTOGRAPHY CREDITS

Sheller; pages 33, 38, 53 (two photos) copyright © by Will Shively; page 54, copyright © by Will Shively; pages 58–59, copyright © by Dede Hatch; pages 62–63, courtesy of Floyd Benzing; page 72, copyright © by Michael J. Epstein; page 73, courtesy of Craig Merrow; pages 74–76, courtesy of David Romtvedt; page 78, courtesy of Rhonda Brittan; pages 85, 92, courtesy of Aaron Ridinger; page 95, courtesy of Jim Howard; page 106, courtesy of Jerry Jess; page 107, copyright © by Michael J. Epstein;

page 108, courtesy of Volkswagen of America; page 113, courtesy of W.W. Fitzpatrick; page 118, copyright © by Will Shively; page 119, copyright © by Neil Johnson; pages 120–121, copyright © by Will Shively; page 122, courtesy of Kevin DeGabriel; page 126 (top left and top right), courtesy of Harrod Blank; page 126 (bottom), copyright © by Eric Staller; page 127, courtesy of Harrod Blank; pages 128–129, copyright © by Steven Grubman; pages 131–132, copyright © by Will Shively; page 133, courtesy of Lois Grace; page 134, courtesy of Volkswagen of America; page 135, courtesy of Catherine Lippert; pages 138–141, copyright © by Michael J. Epstein; page 146, courtesy of Robb White; pages 152–153, copyright © by Michael J. Epstein.

ILLUSTRATION CREDITS
(Credit for artwork paired with essays can be found directly after the author credit for each story.)

Page 78, Map © by C. S. Hammond & Co., N. Y., courtesy of David Romtvedt; page 119, Illustration by William Joyce from his book *Leaf Men*, is reprinted by permission of the author and HarperCollins Books for Children.

With special thanks to Eric Hansen for his wonderful illustrations on pages 10, 11, 26, 55, 65, 90, 97, 116.

Illustrations by Michael J. Rosen appear on pages 13, 78, 82, 83, 84, 85, 97, 123.

Cartoons by Richard Koehler on pages 36, 40, 43, 49, and 89 are reprinted from his chapbook, *Just Plain Volks*, George Griffin Publications, West Carrollton, Ohio, 1958, with thanks to the author.